HOOLIE'S YOOPER JOKE BOOK

Also Featuring:
Dumb Questions Tourists Ask,
Yooper Words of Wisdom and More!

©2015 Yooper Innovations

ISBN: 978-0-9658645-1-0

Library of Congress Control Number: 2014948070

First Edition 2015

10   9   8   7   6   5   4   3   2   1

Published By:
Yooper Innovations, Inc.
490 N. Steel St.
Ishpeming, MI 49849
800-628-9978

Who's On The Cover:
• Richard "Dick-Bird" Bunce
• Jim "Bella" Bellmore
• James "Hoolie" DeCaire

This book is dedicated to all the great Yooper story tellers who I admire for their abilities to tell a funny story: Cully Gage, My Uncle Joe Sarvello, Glenn Adams, Uno Tanskanen and Jerry Harju. Also, thanks to my editor Jesse DeCaire for all his hard work making sense of what I write and arranging it so all of you can understand it.

-Jim "Hoolie" DeCaire

THE OLD LADY AND HER BOAT

One summer, me, Bella and Dicky would go down to Lake Superior to fish for lakers. Everyday when we'd go down to the lower harbor to back the boat in, we would see this older women that was maybe in her 70's also putting her boat in. When we'd return at the end of the day, empty handed, there she would be trailering her boat and without fail she would hold up a whole string of lunkers a mile long for us to see. this went on all summer. Finally, in the fall, I tell Bella to go and ask her what she's using for bait.

"Hell no," Bella exclaimed, "I ain't asking no woman what she uses for bait! That's like, against the yooper laws of manly fishing men or something!"

"Fine," I replied, "I ain't too proud, I'll go ask her." I walked up to her and shook her hand and after a pleasant introduction I launched right into it. "You know, me and my buddies see you here most days and at the end of the day, you've always got your limit caught. Would you mind sharing your secret with me?"

"Oh no I don't mind young man," she said in a thick Keweenaw accent. "Well you see I get up at 5 o' clock AM and make my egg and pepper sandwiches for the day. Then I go and hook up the boat to the jeep and pack all my stuff in the boat. Before I take off I go into the bedroom where my husband Roy is still sawing logs. Then--and this is the key part--I lift up the sheet. If his weiner's laying on his left leg, I fish out the left side of the boat. If it's laying on his right leg, I fish out the right side of the boat. If it's pointing towards his feet, I fish out the back of the boat and if it's pointed at his head, I fish out the front of the boat."

After she was finished, I took a second to take it all in. Then, after some thought I asked, "Yeah, but wonder if it's sticking straight up in the air, what do you do then?"

"Ahh, yes," she replies with a grin, "I stay home."

DICKY FALLS OFF THE WAGON

Dick Bird loved to party but his wife DaLonda didn't like it at all. She hounded him about his drinking day and night, like flies on poop. She always used to say when he would come home tipsy, "If I ever catch you coming home drunk again, I'm gonna drop you like a hot spud!" After many attempts to hide it, Dicky finally gave in and quit going out with the boys. There was just no fooling DaLonda's beagle-like nose, she could smell the beer on his breath even before he stepped into the house.

One night, around six months later, the boys were heading out to Woody's Bar to celebrate No Neck Carlson's birthday. They stopped off at Dicky's to try and persuade him to break his self imposed exile and come out with them.

"Come on Bird," Bruzzy Carlson pleaded, "You gotta come out with us! It's No Neck's birthday and you haven't been out with us in forever! Come on! You can drink a coke or some of that fake beer, just come out with us!" After begging DaLonda and promising her up and down that he would just drink pop she finally caved and let him go out.

It was a different story, however, when they got to Woody's. The minute the smell of stale beer and whiskey hit Dicky's nose, it was all too much for him to handle. His friends were welcoming him back and telling him how good it was to see him and after the tenth person offered to buy him a drink, he caved. "I'll just have one," he told himself. As he held the cool mug of gold liquid in his hand, he was mesmerized by the way the fizzy bubbles darted to the top of the beer and how the beads of condensation ran down the outside of the glass, leaving a trail behind it. "It truly is a thing of beauty" he thought. He closed his eyes as the first gulp of the golden nectar ran down his parched throat. "Ahh yes, now that's gooood." He said to himself.

Around fifteen beers later, Dicky tried to make it to the bathroom in time but ended up throwing up all over himself. He hooked his arm around his friend Mutti Maki for stability and slurred, "Oh god, DaLonda is gonna kill me. She's going to know for sure I've been drinking. What am I gonna do?"

Mutti, feeling his friend's plight, replied, "Eh, Dick Bird, here's what you do. Put ten bucks in your shirt pocket and tell the ol' lady you were drinking a coke when all of a sudden a drunk next to you threw up all over you and he felt so bad that he gave you 10 dollars to get your clothes dry cleaned."

Tears of gratitude welled in Dicky's eyes. "Mutti, you are the smartest guy I know. What you told me just might work!" He gave Mutti a sloppy hug and went back to slamming beers with the boys.

About 3 a.m, Dicky staggered into the house and sure enough there was DaLonda waiting up for him with a cast iron frying pan in her hand (the weapon of choice of all good Yooper women).

"You no good for nothing S.O.B, I knew this was gonna happen if you went out with those no good for nothing bums you call friends. Look at you, you stink of beer and you got puke all over yourself!"

"No, no honey, you got it all wrong," Dick Bird said in his best sober voice. "You see, I was sitting there, drinking a coke, minding my own business when some no good for nothing drunk sitting next to me turned and tossed his cookies all over me! And he felt so bad afterwards that he gave me ten dollars to get my clothes dry cleaned! Reach in my shirt pocket, the money's in dere."

"Hay wait a second," DaLonda said suspiciously, "There's two tens in here, you stooge!"

"Oh yeah, that's right," Dicky looks at her with a sheepish grin, "He pooped in my pants, too."

<hr>

DA PLANE RIDE

Dick Bird and his wife DaLonda go to the U.P State Fair in Escanaba every year and every year he admires the small plane that offers rides for 20 dollars. He pleads with DaLonda to let him take a ride in the plane and every time she replies, "I know you want to go Dick but that ride costs twenty bucks and you know, twenty bucks is twenty bucks."

Finally last year they were there and Dicky spied the same plane offering rides. They walked over so Dicky could ogle the plane and he said, "DaLonda, I'm 71 years old. I've never gotten to ride in an airplane and if I don't do it now, I might never get a chance."

"I know, I know Dicky but it's twenty bucks! And you know, twenty bucks is twenty bucks!"

The pilot just happened to be standing near them and overheard.

"Folks, I've seen you guys come over here every year but never take a ride because its too expensive. Tell you what, I'll make you a deal. I'll take youse both up for a ride and if you can stay quiet for the entire ride and not say one word, I won't charge you the twenty bucks."

Dicky, obviously excited, agreed and dragged DaLonda with him into the plane. Once up in the air, the pilot tries to shake them up by putting the plane through twists and turns, rolls and dives but to his surprise, not a peep came from the back of the plane. He decides to pull out all his best tricks but alas, not a yelp is heard from either Dicky or DaLonda. Defeated, the pilot takes them down and once on the ground he turns around and says to Dicky,

"By golly, I did everything I could think of to shake you two up and get you to yell out but you didn't! I'm impressed!"

"Well," Dicky replied, "I was gonna say something when DaLonda fell out of the plane, but you know, twenty bucks is twenty bucks!"

I Won Da Lottery

Dicky came home from the bar screaming and yelling.

"I WON THE LOTTERY! I WON THE LOTTERY, PACK YOUR BAGS, I WON THE LOTTERY!"

DaLonda, now just as excited as Dicky asks, "What shall I pack for? Warm weather or cold?"

Dicky yells back, elated, "I DON'T CARE! AS LONG AS YOU ARE OUT OF HERE BY NOON!"

Rudy Da Rooster

Dicky had a pet rooster named Rudy. We used to go over to Dicky's and watch him put Rudy through his "paces." He had a little army hat made for him and he would march him around the yard barking, "Left! Right! Left! Right!" and Rudy would keep up! Dick would also have Rudy climb a ladder and have him try to fly off the platform he had built for him. We probably seen Rudy do these tricks a hundred times but they were still funny every time he did them.

One night, Dicky told Dalonda he was going to the Ishpeming Theater to see the new sci-fi movie that was out, "The Eggplant That Ate Chicago."

"You can't go to da movies, Dick," DaLonda said, "I'm going to bingo with mom up in L'Anse and you have to baby sit Rudy while I'm gone."

Dicky was depressed. He really wanted to see that movie and it was the last night that it was showing. Then, in moment of inspiration he thought, "Wait a minute, I'll take Rudy to the theater! He loves sci-fi movies!" So he jumps into the pick-up with Rudy and heads for the movie house. With Rudy under his arm, he walks up to Shirley Maki who was working the ticket booth.

"Two please," Dicky said.

"Oh no, Dick. You can't come in here with that bird. You know no animals are allowed here at the theater."

"Oh come on Shirley!" Dick pleaded. "He's a good rooster, he won't squak or poop on the seats!"

"No, Dicky! Get outta here with that dang bird!" Shirley stood firm.

So Dicky, with his head hanging low headed back to the truck. He didn't stay defeated for long, however. In another moment of inspiration he solved his problem. Since he had on his oversized pants that he got as hand-me-downs from DaLonda's brother No Neck, he had just enough room to hide Rudy down there. So he stuffed him down the waistband and jumped up and down a little to get him settled in there. Dick then pulled out the waistband and said,

"You OK down there Rudy?"

Rudy let out an affimative "SQUAK."

Dick's plan worked like a charm. He got past Shirley and was even able to get a pack of Milk Duds no problem. He found an empty seat next to Gravel Gertie and her chum Olga "Ugga Bug" Stevenson. Dick had to let Rudy out for some air so he waited until the lights went down to unzip his pants. He reached in his fly and fished around until he found Rudy's head. Gertie, watching the whole thing, pokes Ugga and says,

"Hay, Ugga, the guy next to me just unzipped his pants."

"Oh don't pay attention to him," Ugga whispered back, "He's one of those crazy buggers from the neighborhood."

Meanwhile, Dicky found Rudy's head and pulls it out of the opened zipper. Rudy's head darted around and then with eyes like two quarters, fixed on the giant lit up screen which he had never seen before.

Gertie pokes Ugga again. "Ugga, Ugga, now he just pulled his do-hickey out!"

"Oh," Ugga replies with a wave of her hand, "You seen one, you seen 'em all, just don't pay any attention to him."

"No," Gertie said, "This one's different. It's eating my popcorn."

I NEED A PUSH

One cold, snowy, blustery night, me and the wife were settling in for a warm winter's nap, when all of a suden the door bell rings.

"Go see who's at the door at this hour," my wife poked me.

"No way, it can only be trouble," I said burrowing down into the bed. The wife gives me a hefty shove, almost knocking me out of the bed.

"Go see who it is!" She barked again. So I crawl down the stairs swearing under my breath. I open up the door and lo and behold there's my friend Dick Bird standing there loaded to the gills.

"Hay Hoolie, give me a push, eh."

"Oh man, Dick, go home," I say. "It's blowin like heck out there. Just walk home and sleep it off and we can get your car in the morning. Good night." I closed the door on Dick who was wobbling and hiccuping.

"So who was that?" My wife asked when I got back to the bedroom.

"Oh it's just Dick Bird. He needed a push to get his car out of the ditch but there's no way in hell I'm getting dressed up and going out there!"

"Oh you're something else! He's done you a million favors and you shut the door in his face. What kind of neighbor are you?"

What can I say, she was right. "OK, OK I'll go. But I'm not going to like it." I got up begrudgingly and struggled into my snow pants, jacket, boots, "Elmer Fudd" hat and lastly, my choppers. When I opened the door I was immediately hit with a gust of snowy wind and couldn't see two foot in front of me. I started yelling.

"DICKY WHERE ARE YOU?"

"I'm back here!" Oddly, I hear Dicky's faint voice coming from my backyard area. So I start trudging around the house to the backyard.

"DICK! WHERE ARE YOU?" I yelled. "DO YOU STILL NEED A PUSH?"

"Yah I'm back here!" As I rounded the corner of the house I see Dick sitting on my kid's swing set. "Come on over, I need a push!"

Oh I could've killed him. But, being a good friend, I gave him a push.

BELLS AND WHISTLES

One day, Bunna Poleman's kid Jeffery was riding in a little red wagon pulled by his dog Humphrey. He had one end of the rope tied to the wagon handle and the other end attached to Humphrey's nuts.

Dick Bird just happen to be sitting on his porch when he saw Jeffery and Humphrey rolling up the sidewalk. "You know Jeffery," Dick Bird said as they passed by, "If you tie the rope around his neck it would probably go faster."

"I know," Jeffery replied, "But then I wouldn't get the cool siren!"

SMART PILLS

Dick Bird and his son Spags went out south to rabbit hunt with the family beagle Percy. After about an hour they finally come across some rabbit tracks. In between the track, there were little brown pellets and Spags asked his dad:

"What are those?"

"Those are smart pills," Dick said. "Try a couple, they'll make you smarter." So the kid grabbed a couple and put them in his mouth. He scrunched up his face and spit them out.

"Ewww! Yuk! They taste like poop!" The son said scooping up some snow and jamming it into his mouth.

"See, you're getting smarter already!" Dick Bird said, laughing.

Hunting and Fishing

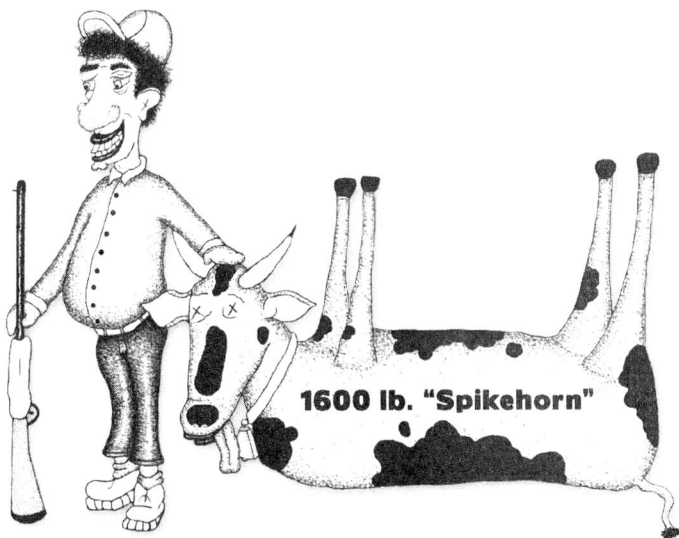

1600 lb. "Spikehorn"

YOOPER GENIE

Me and Bunna were fishing up on the Escanaba River in my boat. It was a typical summer day in Yooperland—hot, muggy and the flies were out in swarms. So, in order help drive away the blood sucking mosquitos, Bunna decides to pull out a massive cigar he was saving for just this kind of occasion.

"Holy wah, where'd you get that huge cigar?" I asked him.

"My brother Jack went down to da Bahamas and smuggled it home in his underwear. It's a real Cuban! You got a light?" Bunna asked.

I reached into my tackle box and pulled out my massive, 12-inch Bic brand lighter and handed it to Bunna.

"Man, where did you get this huge lighter from??" Bunna asked, impressed.

"Oh," I replied, "That's my 12-inch Bic that I got from the little genie that lives in my tackle box!"

Bunna laughs. "Hoolie, you can B.S those trolls that come up to visit The Tourist Trap, but don't try that stuff on me!"

"No, No! It's true! I was up here fishin' with my ma and I see this tackle box come floatin' down the stream. So I start casting at it to try and hook it to see if there's any tackle in there I could use. After the third try I hooked it and reeled 'er in and the minute I put a rag to it to wipe it off, BOOM! Out pops this miniature yooper genie."

"Come on now, Hoolie," Bunna said in disbelief, "This boat is going to sink from all the B.S you're talking!"

"You wanna meet him?" Bunna shakes his head, still skeptical.

I grab the tackle box and started rubbing it with a rag. Then I said my magic chant that went something like this:

> "Yooper Yooper Yooper Genie,
> Come out, Come out You Little Weenie!"

And—POOF! Sure enough, out pops the yooper genie! He had his sagging jeans, a bar jacket, his little baseball cap covered in chainsaw oil and Wellington boots.

"Oh hay Hoolie, what's up?" The genie asks me in his squeaky voice. "Who's this guy?"

"This is my friend Bunna."

"Eh, Bunna, how's about one of them beers you got over there. I get real thirsty livin' in that tackle box, eh!" The genie asks Bunna.

"No little guy, sorry, this is my last one."

"Oh, c'mon! I'll grant you a wish if you throw it my way!"

Bunna thinks on it a minute. "OK, that sounds fair."

"What you want then?"

"Well, I gotta a lotta credit card debt and could use a new car. How about a million bucks?"

"Oh, that's easy. Done!" The genie waves his hand, grabs Bunna's last beer and disappears back into the tackle box.

Bella and I are looking around and nothing seems to be happening.

"Eh, Hoolie, where's my million bucks?" Bunna asks.

"Not sure . . ." And just as I started saying that, the sky got dark and we look up and see a million ducks flying overhead, quacking away.

"Hay!" Bella exclaims. "I asked that little bugger for a million bucks, not a million ducks!"

"Oh," I said, "I forgot to tell you to speak up when you talk to him coz he's hard of hearing. You think I asked him for a 12-inch Bic?"

SAGE DEER CAMP WISDOM

The deer camp is a great place to give and receive advice. Bill Bob and his gramps took a hunting trip out the camp right before Bill Bob was going to marry. Bill Bob asked his gramps what he should expect sex-wise over the years.

"Well, when you're first married, you want it all the time, so you'll end up doing it probably two or three times a day. As time goes on that tapers off to once a week and then once a month until later on in life you're lucky if you do it once a year--maybe on an anniversary or something."

"Where are you at now, gramps?"

"Oh me and your grandma mostly have oral sex now."

"Really, oral sex, well that's OK, I suppose."

"Oh yah just great," Gramps replies sarcastically, "We bicker most nights and I go to one room and she goes to hers and she yells 'SCREW YOU!' and I yell back 'YAH SCREW YOU, TOO!'"

MIRACLES AT DA DEER CAMP

Miracles do happen a lot at the deer camp. Here's one that happened at Camp-Go-For-Beer. We were playing cards one night and there was: Biddo, Mungo, Bella, Bug Eyes, Vito and Gubba. We were having a great time playing poker when Vito all of a sudden says:

"I gotta go to the outhouse. Deal me out."

He heads outside with his long black flashlight and once he got in the can, he sets it down on the side of the hole. He pulls down his hunting bibs and accidentally knocks the flashlight down in the hole and it sticks in the muck facing up while still on. Here's the miracle part: This was the first time in the history of the camp that you could go out to the outhouse, spread your legs and be able to read a magazine! That light stayed on for the whole two weeks of deer season. We had to clean the lens off every once in awhile but it worked great! We wrote EverReady Battery Company our story and how well their batteries worked, thinking they might pick it up for a commercial, but we still haven't heard back from them.

MILLIMAKI'S CAMP

I go to Millimaki's Deer Camp every season. Not to hunt but just to visit with the boys. The camp has been through four generations of hunters and there was one old guy left from the old days that still came out named "Pistol" Pete Petersen who was in his 90's.

The Millimaki's had a couple of their relative's kids up for the hunting season and I was telling them about Pistol Pete and all the good stories he tells. So the two kids go over to Pete who was in the rocking chair snoozing and asked him to tell them a hunting story.

"Go and fetch me a glass of Jim Beam on the rocks and I'll tell you a good hunting story." He croaked to the kids. Once the glass of Beam was in his hand and he took a good pull, he began. "OK young fellas, here's a story that goes all the way back to 1947 here at the camp. We hunted all week with no luck at all—nothing in the swamps, in the woods, over those hills over there—nothing. Eventually I was wore out from all the walking so I found a nice log to sit against and I dozed off. A noise startled me awake and I instinctively reached for my 30-30 when all of sudden this big black bear waltzes right up to me and gives out the loudest roar I've ever heard! It went like ROOAAAAARRRRR-RR!"

After a pause one of the kids asked, "What did you do then?"

"I crapped my pants." Pete replied.

"Well, if a black bear came right up to me and roared in my face I would've crapped my pants too!" The other kid said.

"No, no not then," Pete said, "Just now when I went ROOAAAAAR-RRRRR!"

ALVIN STYLE

Me and Vito were going duck hunting out on Deer Lake. Alvin Maki overheard us and begged us to take him along. We told him to have all his stuff ready to to go at 6 A.M. The next morning, we drive up to his house and he comes out with a fishing pole and a pound of bacon. I look at Vito and we both start laughing.

"Poor Alvin," I said, "If he had a brain he would be dangerous."

"Yah," Vito said, "Going duck hunting with a fishing pole . . . wait 'til the guys here this one."

We don't say anything to him all the way to Deer Lake and we arrive, me and Vito go to the duck blind and leave Alvin to fend for himself.

"Look at those three ducks out in the middle of the lake, guys!" Alvin yells to us after awhile.

"Yah, we see 'em Alvin," Vito says, "They're just too far out to shoot and we don't have a dog to retrieve 'em anyways."

"Oh that's alright, I'll get 'em," Alvin replies.

He takes out the bacon and wraps it around the hook. Then he gives it a mighty cast right out in front of those ducks. The first duck sees the bacon and swims over and gulps it down. A minute later, he poops out the bacon and the next duck comes over and grabs the bacon (still on the hook) and gulps it down. Alvin then starts reeling the two ducks in. Me and Vito were in shock.

One cast and he nabbed 2 ducks! We tossed our guns down and jumped back in the car to go home and grab our poles and some bacon. Ever since then, whenever we duck hunted, we'd leave the guns at home and instead hunted "Alvin-style."

TOILET BEARD

I stopped off at the family bar, The Royal, to see my Uncle Bruno.

"Boy am I glad to see you," he said when he saw me. "Tony just caught a bunch of trout at The Carp and I wanna go fishing. Can you watch the bar for me?"

It seemed pretty slow so I told him I'd cover the bar for a couple of hours. Once I got behind the bar, a real knock-out of a babe signals me to come over to her end of the bar. I go over to her and without a word, she takes my face in her hands and pulls me near her face, running her hands through my beard. Then she starts running her hands through my hair.

"Are you the manager?" She asks in a sultry tone. She had moved her hands back to my beard and was stroking it lightly.

"No, I'm not." I tell her.

"Well, can you get him for me? I really need to speak to him."

"I'm afraid he just left to go fishing and won't be back for a couple of hours." By now I'm totally getting wood because she running her hands through my hair again. "Is there anything I can do for you, m'am?" I ask in an unsteady voice.

"I need you to give him a message," she coos. By this time she's slid a couple of fingers into my mouth and I could barely stand it. "Tell him that there's no toilet paper in the ladies bathroom."

Little Metal Flashlight

Because Michigan is broken up into two peninsulas, people ask all the time what is the difference between a Yooper (someone from the Upper Peninsula) and a Troll (someone from Lower Michigan). Well, here's a story that illustrates that perfectly, a story that comes to you from our deer camp, "Camp-Go-For-Beer."

There were four Troll friends of mine that came up to the camp one hunting season. One day, one of them dropped his two dollar metal flashlight down the outhouse hole while he was trying to read one of those Playboys we had in there. Those guys tried everything to get that flashlight out of there—from fishing poles to long poles with a hook duct-taped to the end. Finally, they drove into town to Jackson's Hardware and bought a magnet and a ball of twine. Then they had to stop off at The Royal Bar for a couple of beers and to chat with my Uncle Bruno. By the time these Trolls got back to camp they had invested about 40 dollars into this two dollar flashlight. Now, here's where the difference comes in. A Yooper wouldn't have bothered with all that stuff the Trolls did, let alone spend more money to get the flashlight out. A Yooper would've looked around the deer camp for the drunkest guy, grab him by the ankles and lower him down the hole to grab that flashlight!

First Buck

Gramps was out in the woodshed when he sees something coming down road, moving side to side. It was hard to make out because the snow was coming down hard but as the figure came closer he realized it was a sight that we rarely saw at our deer camp—a guy dragging a big buck behind him. Gramps runs over and sees that it's Rudy Johnson.

"Holy wah Rudy," Gramps says, "That's a beauty you shot dere."

"Yah," Rudy says, "It's a dandy all right, but I didn't shoot it, Ray did."

"Oh, OK, but say—where is Ray then?"

"He's about three miles back laying on the side of the trail in a snow bank." Rudy says nonchalantly. "He shot this buck and then he grabbed his chest, spun around and flopped in the snowbank. I think he had a coronary or something."

"You mean to tell me you left your best friend laying back dere in the snowbank with a heart attack and you choose to pull the buck back instead?"

"Yah," Rudy said, shaking his head. "It was the hardest decision I had to make in my life, but then I thought, who the hell is going to steal Ray?"

Editor's Note: Ray only had indigestion and came back to the camp after he recovered and danced all night long in celebration of bagging his first buck in 30 years of hunting. He even patted Rudy on the back for making the wise choice.

THE MINE SHAFT

Hoolie and Bunna were out bird hunting when they came upon an old abandoned mine shaft. Curious about how deep it went they threw a rock in and waited for the sound of it hitting bottom but heard nothing. They went and got some bigger rocks, tossed them in and waited . . . still nothing. They searched the area for something larger and came across an old railroad tie. With a lot of grunting they carried it to the opening and tossed it in. While wating for it to hit bottom, a golden retriever suddenly darted between them and jumped into the hole. They stood there mouths agape at what they saw.

"What a crazy dog!" Bunna exclaimed.

A second later, another hunter wandered into the clearing. "Hay fellas, I'm kind of turned around out here and I was wondering if you could help me. You haven't by any chance run across a golden retriever out here have you?"

"Yah," Hoolie replied, "One just ran by us and jumped into that mine shaft over there."

"Oh that couldn't be my dog," the hunter replied, "Mine was tied to an old railroad tie with a real long rope."

The Fishing License

Rainer and Juju were fishing at their special secret spot west of Republic. Out of nowhere, the game warden jumps out of the bushes. Immediately, Rainer tears off running with the game warden hot on his heels, while oddly, Juju slinks back towards the truck in the opposite direction. After about a half mile, Rainer couldn't take it anymore and stopped to catch his breath. As he stood there stooped over with his hands on his knees, the game warden finally caught up, panting heavily.

"Let's see your fishing license, boy!" The game warden barked between gasps. Rainer dug in his wallet and produced a perfectly valid fishing license.

"Well, son," The game warden said a bit puzzled, "You must be dumb as a box of rocks from the Republic Mine! You don't have to run from me if you have a license!"

"Oh yes sir I know," Rainer said, finally catching his breath. "But my friend back there, the one who took off in the truck, well he don't."

The Best Fisherman

Bitto Carlson was the best fisherman in Tangle Town. One day him and his brother Crank go out to his super secret fishing spot to catch some brook trout. Once they got to the lake, Bitto took a stick of dynamite out of his pack sack, lit it and heaved it out to the middle of the lake. BOOM! A second later, a bunch of stunned trout float to the surface.

"Let's Fish!" Bitto exclaimed as he and his brother wade out and proceed to scoop up their easily won booty. When they got back to the truck with their buckets full of fresh live fish, the game warden was waiting for them.

"Finally I got you Bitto! You're going down for this!" He said.

"What do you mean?" Bitto asked calmly.

"Well, I know damn well you don't have a fishing license and you're holding illegally caught fish. You're gonna hang!"

"Wait now a minute there warden," Bitto explained, "Are you talking about these fish? These are my pet fish. I take 'em here so they can get some exercise and a little mating with da udder trout. When it's time to go, all I have to do is whistle and they jump back in da buckets."

"Yah, yah sure," the warden says, "What a crock of bull that is, I've heard 'em all now! Let's go back to the pond, I gotta see this."

Bitto and his brother lug the pails back to the lake and dump them back in.

"Ok, Bitto, whistle and call them back. I wanna see every one of those fish jump back in the buckets."

There was a long silence while Bitto looked around.

"What fish?" He finally replied.

DOWN ON THE FARM

A carload of Yoopers was downstate looking for a place to hunt. They found a farm just off of I-75 and pulled into the yard. Rudy went up to the house to ask the farmer permission to hunt on his land. The farmer was agreeable.

"Sure you can hunt here but would you do me a favor? That old mule standing over there is 20 years old and sick with cancer but I don't have the heart to kill her. Would you do it for me?"

Feeling obligated to the nice farmer, Rudy replied, "Sure I will," and headed back to car for his gun. While en route, he decides to play a trick on his hunting buddies. He got into the car and when they asked if the farmer said it was OK, he said, "He said we can't hunt here but I'm gonna teach that old coot a lesson." With that he rolled down his window, stuck his gun out and blasted the mule. "There that'll teach him!"

And just as he said that a second shot rang out from the backseat and Roy, his hunting buddy exclaimed, "I got the cow!"

WHAT ARE WE EATING?

Pink Anderson kills a deer and brings it home. He decides to clean it and serve the venison for supper. He knows his kids are fussy eaters and won't eat it if they know what it is, so he decides not to tell them. His little boy keeps asking him, "What's for supper, dad?" and Pinky tells him each time:

"You'll see! Just hold your horses!" Suppertime rolls around and the venison is served. To his joy, Pinky sees his kids eating the venison but the daughter is relentless.

"Dad, what are we eating? Dad, what are we eating?" Finally Pinky couldn't take it anymore.

"Ok, ok. I'll give you a hint," he says still weary about telling them, "It's what your mother sometimes calls me."

The daughter spits the meat out and screams, "We're eating asshole??!"

ICE ICE BABY

Three dudes from Lower Michigan love to fish. So they decide they want to try ice fishing since they had heard so many good things about it. Because the ice was piss poor in southern Michigan, the Three Amigos head up north, across the Big Mac Bridge to Yooperland. Once they get near the Little Bay De Noc River, they stop off at Bill's Bait Shop to get all their tackle and gear, including a spud to chop through the ice.

About two hours later, one of them was back at the Bait Shop and said to Bill, "We're going to need another spud." With a new spud in tow, the city slicker heads back out to his buddies on the ice. Another hour goes by, the same guy walks into Bill's again and says, "We're gonna need another spud." Well, at this point, Bill couldn't take it anymore, he needed to know.

"By the way," he says after selling the guy another spud, "How are you fellas doing out there?"

"Not very well at all," the Troll replies, "We don't even have the stupid boat in the water yet."

The Boat Rental

U-bolt and Eye-Bolt Carlson were identical twin brothers. U-bolt owned an old dilapidated boat and kept pretty much to himself. One day he rented out his boat to a group of trolls from down below who ended up sinking it. He spent all day trying to salvage as much stuff as he could from the sunken vessel and was out of touch all that day and most of the evening. Unbeknownst to him, his brother Eye-Bolt's wife had died suddenly in his absence.

When he got back on shore he went into town to pick up a few things at the IGA Grocery Store. He ran into Bertha Anderson who mistook him for him for Eye-Bolt and said, "I'm so sorry for your loss. You must feel terrible."

U-Bolt, thinking she was talking about his boat said, "Hell no! Fact is I'm sort of glad to be rid of her. She was a rotten old thing from the beginning. Her bottom was all shriveled up and she smelled like old dead fish. She was always holding water. She had a bad crack in the back and a pretty big hole in the front too. Every time I used her, her hole got bigger and she leaked like crazy. I guess what finally finished her off was when I rented her to those four apple knockers looking for a good time. I warned them that she wasn't very good and that she smelled bad. But they wanted her anyway. The damn fools tried to get in her all at one time and she split right up the middle."

Old Lady Anderson couldn't believe her ears and fainted right on the spot.

Lists

A – as in: "You betcha, 'A'!"
B – as in: "I yoosta 'B,' not any more, doh..."
C – as in: "'C,' I told you to buy more beer."
D – as in: "I'm gonna fix da roof one a' 'D's' days..."
E – as in: "Eeeee, dat pasty's hot!"
F – as in: "I got a 'F' in algebra"
G – as in: "G'dat beer was good!"
H – as in: "I had my first beer at the 'H' of 13..."
I – as in: "I like beer!"
J – What my hippie uncle smokes.
K – Answer da wife: "'K,' I'll get to da snow shoveling later..."
L – as in: "What da 'L'?"
M – as in: "I 'M' too a good shot!"
N – as in: "I went to da camp 'N' pairted."
O – as in: "'O' I didn't know dat."
P – as in: "Pull over, I gotta take a 'P.'"
Q – as in: "I sank da 'Q' ball..."

R – as in: "'R' you ready?"
S – as in: "I slipped and fell on my 'S.'"
T – What dem English people drink.
U – as in: "'U' better listen!"
V – What da geese in da sky fly in.
W – as in: "I saw 'U' at da bar and after 20 beers I saw 'W's!'"

X – as in: "Da 'X' left me for a rich Troll."
Y – as in: "'Y' you say dat?"
Z – as in: "Let's go 'Z' camp."

THE YOOPERLAND MY FAULT INSURANCE CO.

These are actual statements found on insurance forms where drivers attempted to summarize the details of an accident in the fewest words possible. This goes to show you that faulty writing can be entertaining!

1. An invisible car came out of nowhere, struck my car and vanished.
2. I told the police that I was not injured but when I removed my hat, I found that I had a fractured skull.
3. My car was legally parked as it backed into the other vehicle.
4. Coming home, I pulled into the wrong house and collided with a tree I don't have.
5. I thought my window was down but I found it was up when I put my hand through it.
6. I collided with a stationary truck coming the other way.
7. A pedestrian hit me and went over my car.
8. The guy was all over the road. I had to swerve a number of times before I hit him.
9. I pulled away from the side of the road, glanced at my mother-in-law and headed over the embankment.
10. In my attempt to kill a fly, I drove into a telephone pole.
11. I had been driving for 40 years when I fell asleep at the wheel and had an accident.
12. To avoid hitting the bumper of the car in front of me, I struck the pedestrian.
13. I was sure the old fellow would never make it to the other side of the road when I struck him.
14. The pedestrian had no idea which direction to run, so I ran over him.
15. The telephone pole was approaching and I was attempting to swerve out of its way, when it struck my front end.
16. I was thrown from my car as it left the road. I was later found in a ditch by some stray cows.
17. I saw a slow moving, sad-faced gentleman as he bounced off the hood of my car.

Shirley Kempanen's Words of Wisdom

1. I was thinking if mosquitos only sucked fat instead of blood in the U.P, we would all be skinny.
2. If we're not meant to have a midnight snack, why is there a light in the fridge?
3. I thought I was having a hot flash this morning and then I realized it was just my boobs in my coffee!
4. Marriage is like a deck of cards. In the beginning, all you need is two hearts and a diamond. By the end, you wish you had a club and a spade!
5. You know your life has changed when going to the grocery store by your self is a vacation.
6. We'll be friends 'til we're old and senile, then we'll be new friends!
7. You never truly understand something until you can explain it to your grandmother.
8. Children seldom misquote you. In fact, they usually repeat word for word what you shouldn't have said.
9. The fastest way to a man's heart is through the chest wall with a sharp knife.
10. Female black widow spiders kill the males after mating to stop the snoring before it starts
11. I never knew what real happiness was until I got married—then it was too late.
12. Men were given larger brains than dogs so they won't hump your leg at a cocktail party.
13. The only thing I have in common with my husband is that we were married on the same day.
14. Sex is hereditary. If your parents didn't have it, chances are you won't either.
15. Girls get minks the same way minks get minks
16. Men are like wine. They start out like grapes and it's our job to stomp on them and keep them in the dark until they mature into something we'd like to have dinner with.
17. A man who has lost 75% of his intelligence is called DIVORCED.

GLENN ADAMS WORDS OF WISDOM

1. Some days you're the dog, somedays you're the hydrant.
2. I finally got my head together, now my body is falling apart.
3. Funny, I don't remember being absent-minded.
4. If God wanted me to touch my toes, he would have put them on my knees.
5. Old people shouldn't eat health foods. They need all the preservatives they can get.
6. If you look like your passport picture, you probably need the trip.
7. Never put both feet in your mouth at the same time because then you don't have a leg to stand on.
8. The only reason I would take up exercising is so that I could hear heavy breathing again.
9. I have to exercise early in the morning before my brain figures out what I'm doing.
10. The advantage of exercising every day is that you die healthier.
11. When everything is coming your way, you're in the wrong lane.
12. I used to have an open mind but my brains kept falling out.
13. Never play leapfrog with a unicorn.
14. If a man is in the forest talking to himself with no women around, is he still wrong?
15. If a woman is in the forest talking to herself with no man around, is she still complaining?
16. Did you know the shortest sentence in the English language is "I am?" The longest: "I do."
17. I saw two horseflies in the kitchen today, both females. How did I know? They were both on the phone.
18. Very few things upset my wife and it makes me feel special to be one of them.
19. Women are always complaining that they want men who are sensitive, caring and good looking. Hell, all these men already have boyfriends!
20. Did you know there are female hormones in beer? You drink a lot of beer and you end up getting fat, you talk too much and don't make sense, you cry and you can't drive a car!

DUMB QUESTIONS TOURISTS ASK

Here at Da Yoopers Tourist Trap we get a lot of emails asking us some pretty out there stuff about the U.P. So, being the "serious" information source that we are, of course we're going to give them the "correct" answers to their questions! Believe it or not these are actual questions people have sent us!

Tourist: Will I see Moose in the streets?

Da Yoopers: Depends on how much beer you drink.

Tourist: Which direction is north in the U.P?

Da Yoopers: Face south, turn to your left 90 degrees, then call us for the rest of the directions when you get there.

Tourist: Can you bring cutlery into the U.P?

Da Yoopers: Why? Just use your fingers like we do.

Tourist: Are there supermarkets in the U.P and is milk available?

Da Yoopers: No we are a peaceful people of vegan hunter/gatherers. Milk is illegal.

Tourist: Are there any ATM machines in the U.P?

Da Yoopers: No but any trading post will give you money for furs.

Tourist: Do you have hotels or motels where we can stay?

Da Yoopers: No, but you can rent a tent from any trading post. They'll also throw in a guide for an extra five bucks.

Tourist: I have question about a certain U.P animal: I've heard it's like a big horse with horns. What is it?

Da Yoopers: It's called a moose. They're tall and very violent. They're known to eat the brains of anyone walking near them.

Tourist: I've heard moose can be very dangerous if you meet one in the woods. What can be done to distract them should that happen?

Da Yoopers: Spray yourself with human urine before you go out. That always works for us.

Tourist: Do you have wood and brick houses in the U.P?

Da Yoopers: No we actually live in igloos. Mine has two stories!

Tourist: Do y'all have pets up there?

Da Yoopers: Yah, I had a pet beaver named Chompy, but he died. Now I got a bobcat to replace him.

Tourist: Please send a list of doctors in the U.P that dispense rattlesnake bite serum.

Da Yoopers: No need. All the U.P rattlesnakes are harmless. It's the snow snakes that can kill you!

Tourist: At what time does the Mackinaw Bridge swing over to Mackinaw Island so we can go over there?

Da Yoopers: 10:30 am, 1:30 pm and 5:00 pm

Tourist: When do you turn on the Northern Lights?

Da Yoopers: If you want to see the Northern Lights, drive 15 miles north of County Road ZZG. At the end of ZZG you'll find an old bush road. Turn left, and go 12 miles until you see a log cabin. Jenny and Bill Johnson there and operate the generator. Bring a 12-pack for payment but pay after they turn the lights on.

Tourist: Do you accept American currency in the U.P?

Da Yoopers: You may have your American currency exchanged for Yooper Cash at any trading post.

Tourist: Do you have paved roads in the U.P?

Da Yoopers: Yes, but only for the tourists. Most of us locals Kayak or use dog sleds in the winter to get to work.

Tourist: How do the deer know they're supposed to cross the highway at the "Deer Crossing" signs?

Da Yoopers: Just like apes are taught things like simple human functions like shape recognition, yooper deer have been painstakingly trained to recognize those signs. It was part of a safe driving initiative by former Governor Jennifer Grandholm.

DA YOOPERS SCHOOL FOR THE TRULY UNGIFTED FOOTBALL PLAYER ELIGIBILITY TEST

1. What language is spoken in France?

2. What religion is The Pope? (Circle one)
    a) Jewish   b) Catholic   c) Hindu   d) Polish   e) Agnostic

3. What time is it when the big hand is on the 12 and the little hand is on the 5?

4. How many Commandments was Moses given approximately?

5. Where does rain come? (Circle one)
    a) Macy's   b) 7-11   c) Canada   d) The Sky

6. Can you explain Einstein's Theory of Relativity? (Circle one)
    a) Yes   b) No

7. The Star Spangled Banner is the National Anthem for what country?

8. Where is the basement in a three story building located?

9. Which part of America produces the most oranges? (Circle one)
    a) New York   b) Florida   c) Canada   d) Michigan

10. If you have three apples, how many apples do you have?

11. What does NBC (National Broadcasting Corporation) stand for?

12. What are people in America's far north called? (Circle one)
    a) Westerners   b) Easterners   c) Southerners   d) Northerners

DA YOOPERS NEWS WEEKLY

ISHPEMING - A plane crash occured yesterday north of Ishpeming. The U.P news media has labeled it as Northern Michigan's worst air disaster. The plane, a small, two seat Cessna 152 went down in the Ishpeming Cemetery sometime around 10 AM. Rudy and Ray Carlson, working as the Yooper Volunteer Search and Rescue Team, have recovered 256 bodies so far and expect the number to climb as digging continues into the evening.

REPUBLIC - Three major archaeological discoveries about our communication systems have rocked the scientific world just in the past month, one even happening right here in Yooperland. The first happened on the east coast where scientists from New York University, having dug to a depth of 1000 feet in an old colonial settlement, found traces of copper wire dating back over two hundred years and have come to the conclusion that our predecessors already had a telephone network in place much earlier than we'd originally thought.

Not long after that discovery, Archaeologists working on a site in the deserts of Arizona, found similar copper wire that dated to 100 years before that found in New York and they think that its possible that the Native Americans who settled there were far more advanced in their communication systems that we had originally thought.

Hearing about these first two discoveries, Yooper Archaeologist Rudy Kempanen decided to check some of the known early settlements near Republic. Rudy's dig produced no such traces and he deduced from his findings that over 300 years ago, far earlier than that of the New York and Arizona site discoveries that Yooperland had already gone wireless!

"Everyone is always saying Yoopers are behind the technological curve," Kempanen was quoted as saying after the dig. "This proves otherwise."

MARQUETTE - A teen who tried to copy a scene from the hit film "American Pie" by "shagging" a pasty pie was rushed to the hospital with serious burns to his genital region. Dwight Umberger, 17, couldn't wait for the pasty to cool down and was badly scalded by the hot filling. A hospital spokesman said:

"This demonstrates that movie makers should consider the effects their movies have on young and impressionable people."

ISHPEMING - Three men from Ishpeming in a pickup truck skidded off the Carp River Bridge into the river at approximately 7 pm last night. Gubba Olsen, 51, was driving and managed to get the window down and swim to safety. The other two men in the truck, Hack Warra, 47 and Phyko Erickson, 45, both of Rumley, were in the back of the open pick-up truck and drowned. Police said that it looked like they died trying to get the tail gate down.

NEGAUNEE - Police were called the other night around 10:30 by Toivo Millimaki who said he noticed a couple of guys lurking around his back barn. Police told Mr. Millimaki that there wasn't anyone available at that moment to respond but they would send someone out as soon as they were available. About five minutes later, police received another phone call from Mr. Millimaki this time stating that he no longer needed the police because he had shot the perpetrators. Police immediately dispatched all cars in the vicinity of Millimaki's property, plus a helicopter and an armed response unit. When they arrived on site, they found two men in the barn in the process of stealing Tovio Millimaki's stores of raw copper ore. One of the police officers on site was overheard questioning Mr. Millimaki about the incident.

"I thought you said you shot the two men that were in your barn?" The Police officer asked.

"And I thought youse told me there were no cops available," Toivo said with smirk.

IRON MOUNTAIN - A strange new trend is developing at the workplace—people naming food that's put in the communal fridge at their work. Alma Maki reports that she ate a pasty named Kevin just the other day and it was delicious.

10 COMMON YOOPER FISHING TERMS

<u>Catch and Release</u>: A conservation motion that happens most often right before the local DNR Officers pull over a boat full of yoopers that has caught over the limit.

<u>Hook</u>: A curved piece of metal used to catch fish
2. A clever advertisement to entice yooper fishermen to spend his life savings on a new rod and reel.
3. The punch administered by said fishermen's wife after he spends their life savings.

<u>Line</u>: Something you give your co-workers when they ask on Monday how your fishing went the past weekend.

<u>Lure</u>: An object that is semi-enticing to fish but will drive an angler into a frenzy when he charges his credit card to the limit before exiting the sports shop.

<u>Reel</u>: A weighted object that causes a rod to sink quickly when dropped over board.

<u>Rod</u>: An attractively painted length of fiberglass that keeps an angler from ever getting too close to da fish.

<u>School</u>: A grouping in which fish are taught to avoid your 29.99 lures and hold out for spam instead.

<u>Tackle</u>: What your last catch did to you as you reeled him in but just before he wrestled free and jumped back overboard.

<u>Tackle Box</u>: A box shaped like a first aid kit, only a tackle box contains many sharp objects so that when you reach in the wrong box blindly to get a band aid, you soon find that you need more than one.

<u>Test</u>: The amount of strength a fishing line affords an angle when fighting fish in a specific weight range.
2. A measure of your creativity in blaming that blood line for once again losing a fish.

Yooper Comedian Don Ricklamaki's one liners for beginners

My best friend ran away with my wife. It's only been three days and I really miss him.

A man inserted an ad in the classifieds: "Wife wanted." The next day he received a hundred letters. They all said the same thing: "You can have mine."

One of my pet peeves is women who don't put the toilet seat back up when they're finished.

My wife would be a success on the parole board. She never lets anyone finish a sentence.

My doctor was right when he said he'd have me walking in no time. When I got his bill I had to sell my car to pay it!

I've lost my mind and I'm pretty sure my kids took it.

I don't worry about terrorism, I was married for 20 years.

A healthy nap not only makes your life longer, it also shortens the work day.

This year, the immigration department will start deporting senior citizens instead of illegal immigrants in order to lower social security and medicare costs. Older folks are easier to catch and are less likely to remember how to get home!

My wife is an earth sign. I'm a water sign. Together we make mud.

When I die I want to go peacefully like my Uncle Uno did. Not yelling and screaming like the passengers in his car.

It's not that I'm afraid of dying, it's just that I don't want to be there when it happens.

A YOOPERLAND GUIDE TO THE COLD WINTER WEATHER

60 Degrees Above Zero: People in Hawaii turn on the heat. People in Da U.P plant gardens.

32 Degrees Above Zero: People in Florida put on coats, scarves, gloves, long johns and wool hats. People in the U.P put on flannel shirts.

15 Degrees Above Zero: People in New York start turning up the heat in their houses. Yoopers have a last barbeque before it gets cold.

Zero: People in Miami start to perish. Yoopers start closing their windows.

10 Below Zero: People in California start flying down to Mexico and South America. Yoopers start getting out their winter coats.

25 Below Zero: Los Angeles declares a state of emergency and completely shuts down. The Girl Scouts in Ishpeming are selling cookies door to door.

40 Below Zero: People in Georgia's pipes start bursting because they're unprepared. Meanwhile in Yooperland, people finally start letting their dogs sleep inside.

100 Below Zero: Santa Claus Abandons the North Pole and decides to move his operation to the Bahamas. Yoopers are pissed because the truck won't start in the morning.

459.67 Below Zero (Absolute Zero): All atomic motion stops. Yoopers start saying, "Oh yah, is it cold enuff for yuh, dere pretty much?"

500 Below Zero: Hell freezes over. Yooper schools delay school two hours in the morning.

SHIRLEY'S DIET TIPS FOR YOUNG WOMEN

If you eat something and no one else see you eat it, it has no calories.

When drinking diet pop while eating a chocolate bar, the calories in the bar are cancelled out by the diet pop.

When you eat with someone else, calories don't count as long as you don't eat more than they do.

Foods used for medicinal purposes like hot chocolate, brandy, toast and cheesecake never count.

If you fatten up everyone else around you, then you look thinner.

Movie related foods like Milk Duds and Buttered popcorn don't have any calories because they are technically classified under the entire entertainment package and not part of one's personal fuel.

Cookie pieces contain no calories because the process of breaking the cookie causes sufficient calorie burn to cancel it out.

If you are in the process of preparing something, foods licked off of knives and spoons have no calories, again because the activity cancels the calories out.

Foods the same color have the same number of calories. For example, green salad and key lime pie. mushrooms and white chocolate to name a few.

If you eat the food off someone else's plate, it doesn't count.

If you eat standing up, the calories all go to your feet and get walked off.

Food eaten at Thanksgiving and Christmas don't count because they are part of the "holiday season" therefore it's seperate from normal, everyday life.

GUMMER'S LIST OF THINGS YOU'LL NEVER HEAR A YOOPER DUDE SAY

1. "I just love how Barry Manilow sings, don't you?"

2. "No, I don't want another beer. I have to work tomorrow."

3. "You know, her boobs are just too big for my liking."

4. "Sometimes, I just wanna be held."

5. "Sure, honey! I'd be happy to discuss the state of our relationship!"

6. "We haven't been to the mall in ages. Let's go shopping and I can hold your purse."

7. "Forget Monday Night Football. Let's watch something meaningful on the Hallmark Channel."

8. "It's late. Put your clothes back on and I'll take you home."

9. "Honey, I'm going to the store. Do you need more tampons?"

10. "Actually, I prefer it when you hold the remote."

11. "I'm sick of beer. Throw me one of those Capri Suns."

12. "Great! Your mother is coming to stay with us!"

13. "No, no, no. You weeded the garden last week. It's my turn!"

14. "Better get rid of these old Hustler's. I don't look at them anymore."

15. "I understand."

16. "This movie has way too much gratuitous nudity."

17. "Damn these onions! Pass me a tissue."

18. "Eat something for pete's sake! You're starting to look like a Victoria's Secret Model!"

19. "Don't pick that up, I got it."

20. "Happy Anniversary!"

21. "Hey, isn't today your mother's birthday?"

22. "Let's talk. I miss talking."

23. "I am just too tired to have sex again today!"

24. "Are you losing weight, sweetie?'

GLEN ADAM'S SIGNS YOU AND DA WIFE ARE GETTING TOO OLD DERE, PRETTY MUCH

1. Your houseplants are alive and you can't smoke any of them.

2. You keep more food than beer in da fridge.

3. 6 AM is when you get up, not when you go to bed.

4. You hear your favorite song in an elevator.

5. You watch the Weather Channel.

6. Your friends marry and divorce instead of hook up and break up.

7. You're the one calling the police because of those darn kids next door won't turn down that music!

8. You don't know what time Taco Bell closes but you know what time Burger King opens.

9. Dinner and a movie is the whole date instead of the beginning of one.

10. You actually eat breakfast food at breakfast time.

11. You go to the drug store for Metamucil and Ibuprofen, not condoms and pregnacy tests.

12. You feed da dog actual dog food instead of Mcdonald's leftovers.

Old Man Niemi Remembers The 1950s

Here's a list of things that Old Man Niemi remembers people saying in the 50s

"If things keep going the way they are, its going to be impossible to buy a week of groceries for 20 bucks!"

"If cigarettes keep going up in price, I'm going to quit. A quarter a pack is too much."

"Did you hear the post office is thinking about charging a dime just to mail a letter?"

"If they raise the minimum wage to 1 dollar, nobody will be able to afford to hire outside help at their stores!"

"I can't believe the kids today with those long duck tail haircuts. Next, boys will be wearing their hair as long as girls!"

"Society's standards are going down the tubes. Ever since they let Clark Gable say 'damn' in 'Gone With The Wind,' it seems every Hollywood movie has a 'hell' or a 'damn' in it!"

"When we first started driving, who would've ever thought that one day gas would cost as much as 29 cents a gallon!"

"No one can afford to be sick anymore. 35 dollars a day in the hospital is too rich for my blood!"

"Times are getting tough. I've heard that in some families, some of the married women have to work to make ends meet!"

"I never thought I'd see the day when all of our appliances would be electric. They're even making an electric typewriter!"

Shirley's Guide To Yooper Etiquette For Guys

If you and the wife run out of gas, it is impolite to ask her to bring back some beer when you send her down the road with the gas can.

Dim your headlights for approaching vehicles, even if the gun is loaded and the deer is in sight.

When making dinner for a first date, the centerpiece for the table should never be anything prepared by a taxidermist

Always offer to bait your date's hook, especially on the first date.

If your dog falls in love with your date's leg, have the decency to leave them alone for a few minutes.

Change your sheets often, especially if you're expecting company. If you have to use a vacuum on the bed, it's a little too late.

While ears need to be cleaned regularly, as a rule, it should be done in private and with one's own truck keys.

Never let the dog eat at the table, no matter how good his manners are.

Underwear should be changed daily, except when out at deer camp, which can be changed once every week or so.

When bringing a date to a movie, refrain from talking to the characters on screen. Studies have proven that they cannot hear you.

Neighborhood Characters

Ubolt and EyeBolt Carlson

Two yooper brothers, U-Bolt and Eye-Bolt Carlson, were the bullies of the town. One night, they were driving home from the Pine Grove Bar, plastered, when they skidded off the road and into a rock pile on the side of the road. The next thing they know, they wake up in Hell. After stumbling around the fiery inferno for awhile, the brothers find a fire to warm up by. The Devil eventually appears before them and seeing them dressed in their parkas, bomber hats and choppers asks:

"What do you two think you're doing? Isn't it hot enough here in Hell for ya?"

U-Bolt responds, "Vell, ya know dere Mister Devil, we're from Nordern Michigan, the land of snow and ice and cold. We're just happy for a chance to warm up a little bit ya know."

The Devil decides that these two don't seem miserable enough so he takes his leave and turns the heat up in Hell. After awhile, he returns to check and see how they are doing and again he's greeted with the two brothers dressed in their parkas, bomber hats and choppers. The Devil, dumbfounded, asks: "It's awful hot in here, can't you guys feel that at all?"

Eye-Bolt responds this time. "Vell, like we said before, we're from Nordern Michigan, the land of snow and ice and cold, so we're just happy for a chance to warm up a vee bit, ya know."

This gets the Devil quite steamed so he decides to fix these two once and for all. He stokes the deepest darkest fires of Hell really good and cranks the thermostat in Upper Hell as high as it will go. At this point, all the other people banished to Hell are wailing and screaming everywhere. With a satisfied grin, the devil returns to the two yooper brothers and finds them at the same fire, this time with their Detroit Lions sweatshirts and their parkas on the ground. They were grilling some walleye on the fire and drinking a couple of beers. The Devil is shocked.

"Everyone else here is in abject misery," The Devil bellows, "And you two seem to be enjoying yourselves! What gives?"

U-Bolt pipes up. "Vell, ya know, we don't get too much varm vetter up dere in da U.P. We just love to have a fish fry when the vetter's dis nice!"

The Devil at this point is so furious, he can hardly see straight. Finally, he comes up with the answer he was looking for. "These two yoopers love the heat," he thinks, "Because they've been freezing cold all their life. All I have to do to make them miserable is to turn all the heat off in Hell!" So, as quick as he can, he extinguishes all the fires in Hell and turns the heat completely off on Upper Hell's thermostat. The temperature soon drops down to 40 below and icicles start forming everywhere. An eerie silence descends on Hell because people are now cold and shivering so much that they can no longer wail and gnash their teeth. The Devil now thinks he has the brothers right where he wants them, so he returns the small room where he left them. He finds them back in their parkas, bomber hats and choppers, jumping up and down, yelling and cheering like mad men.

The Devil throws his hands up in despair. "I don't understand. When I turn up the heat, you two are happy. Now it's freezing cold and you're happy. What the hell is wrong with you two? Please, I must know!"

The brothers look back at The Devil in surprise. "Vell," Eye-Bolt responds, "Don't ya know, we always heard that if Hell froze over dat must mean Da Lions must've won Da Super Bowl!"

YOOPERS IN VEGAS

3 guys from The Mine, Roy, Pete and Bucko take their wives to Las Vegas for a long weekend. When they get back to work, they started reminiscing about the trip when they were on their lunch break.

"I don't think I'll do that again," Roy says, "Ever since we got back, the wife has been yelling '7 COME 11' in her sleep and flailing her arms around all night long and I can't get no sleep."

"Yah, same with me!" Pete responds. "The ol' lady plays Blackjack in her sleep and is constantly yellin' 'HIT ME, HIT ME HARD!' I can't get no sleep neither."

Bucko balks. "You think youse got it bad. My wife played the slots the whole time in Vegas and now I wake up every morning with a sore johnson and my bum full of quarters!"

FRANKIE AND BRUNO

My uncle Bruno was working one end of the bar at The Royal Bar in Ishpeming and my uncle Frankie was working the other end. There were only two guys sitting at the bar in front of Bruno. One of the guys turns to the other and says:

"I can't help but think from listening to you talk, you must be a true yooper."

"Yah dat's for sure, eh!" The other guy responds proudly.

"Holy wah! So am I! Where abouts are you from?" The first guy asks.

"Republic." The other guy answers.

"Holy crap, I'm from Republic! What street you live on?"

"Oak Street."

"Man, I live on Oak street!" The first guy exclaims. "I wonder why I've never seen you! Did you go to school in Republic?"

"Oh yah, I went to Republic High School."

"Dat's so funny, so did I! What year did you graduate?"

"Well now, let's see, I graduated in 1964."

"God must be looking down on us and smiling," the guy says with his hands up looking toward the ceiling, "I can hardly believe our good luck at winding up in the same bar tonight. Can you believe it? I myself graduated from Republic High School in 1964!"

At this point my uncle Frankie goes over to Uncle Bruno, who had been listening to the whole conversation between the two guys. "How are things going down here?"

"It's going to be a long night tonight," Bruno replies, rolling his eyes, "The Sullivan twins are drunk again."

THREE GIRLS

Tommy Toumainen walks into The City Drug Store and whispers to Jackie Johnson, the pharmacist. "Listen. I have 3 girls coming over tonight and I've never had 3 girls at once.

Jackie rolls her eyes and reaches down and comes up with a small packet. "Yah," she says sarcastically, "You are some lucky bugger. Here, take this pill here. It's Viagra Extra Strength. One of these will make you like Superman for 12 hours."

The next day, Tommy comes into the drug store and walks up to Jackie and pulls down his pants. Jackie looks in horror at Tommy's member which is black and blue and marked up. "I need a bottle of Bengay, please."

"Bengay?!" Jackie replies. "You're not going to put Bengay on your piece while its in that condition are you?"

"No," Tommy replied, "It's for my arms. The 3 girls never showed up."

TRIP TO THE DENTIST

Toivo and Martha Maki went to the dentist to see about getting a tooth pulled. Once they were shown into Doc Frounfelter's office Toivo made it clear:

"I don't wanna spend too much money, so no fancy stuff, Doc. No gas, no needles or any stuff like that. Just pull the tooth and get it over with."

"I wish more of my paitients were as stoic as you," Doc Frounfelter said patting Toivo on the shoulder in admiration. "Now, which tooth is it?"

Toivo turned to his wife. "Show him your tooth, honey!"

FASCINATE

I remember being in school with some of the craziest buggars growing up. One of the craziest by far was Alvin Swanson. Alvin wasn't, shall we say, "rowing his boat with both oars." One day in 4th grade, our teacher Ms. Norman was giving us vocabulary words and we had to make up a sentence as fast as we could. She called on Alvin who jumped up and stood at attention like he was in the army.

Alvin was looking up and down and then closed his eyes like he was thinking real hard and finally said, "OK, I got it, here goes. My sister has a sweater that has 10 buttons on it but her boobs are so big she can only fasten-eight."

CAN YOU SPELL THAT?

Bucko Lehto calls Fassbender's Funeral Home. Old Man Fassbender answers the phone.

"Can I help you?" He says into the phone.

"Yah," Bucko replies, "my ol' lady croaked last night. Can you come pick her up?"

"Well, first you gotta get a doctor over dere to pronounce her dead."

"Oh," Bucko says, "I already did that. Doc Bertucci was here and he told me to call you."

"OK, we'll be over in a jiffy. Where do you live?"

"Eucalyptus Street, last house on the left."

"How do you spell that?" Old Man Fassbender asked.

"U-C. No, no. U-C-A. No that's not right. Y-U-C-A.....hey, how about I drag her carcass over to Oak Street and you can pick her up there if that's OK...That's Oak, O-A-K."

GUBBA IN HEAVEN

Gubba Benson finds himself at the Pearly Gates of Heaven. St. Peter is standing at his podium in front of the gates and asks him for his name.

Gubba, still confused and looking around, sheepishly approaches the podium. "My name is Billy 'Gubba' Benson, sir," he says taking his Elmer Fudd hat off.

"Let me check my good book for your name," St. Peter replies. "Ahh, well, I'm looking at your record and I'm not seeing one good deed that you performed while you were on Earth."

"Wait a minute dere St. Pete, no offense, but I beg to differ. What about that time I was driving down the road and I saw that KKK biker gang hassling that young innocent girl and I went up to the leader who had dat chain from his nose to his ear and ripped out the chain and beat him with a tire iron? And then remember the rest of the bikers circled me and I yelled:

"You are all sick, deranged animals! Go home before I teach you all a lesson in pain!"

"Well," St. Peter said, impressed. "When did all that happen?"

"Oh, about 2 minutes ago."

THE YOOPER PICASSO

We have a great yooper painter not far down the road in Humbolt named Marvin Ruspakka. One day he was in his barn which was also his painting studio, working on a piece when a brand new Cadillac pulled up. A well dressed, good looking woman got out and walked into Marvin's studio and introduced herself.

"I'm Jennifer Oxnard from Chicago visiting a friend who has one of your paintings and I love it! I'm willing to pay you 10,000 dollars if you'll paint me in the nude."

Marvin couldn't believe it, it was the most he'd ever been offered yet for one of his paintings. "Well," he said still flabbergasted, "I would love to, but let me go ask my wife first to see if it's OK with her." Five minutes later Marvin returns to the women. "She says it's OK. Now that I'm gonna paint you in the nude, you think it will be OK if I leave my socks on? I need something to wipe my paint brushes on."

CLOSE DA GARAGE DOOR

Mutti walks into work one morning not knowing his zipper was down and his barn door was wide open. When he was passing his assistant Shirley's desk, she turned and asked:

"When you left your house this morning did you remember to close your garage door?"

"Yah, I did," Mutti said, puzzled by the question.

It wasn't until the middle of the day when he suddenly and with dread realized his fly had been open the entire day and he quickly zipped it up. It then dawned on him what his assistant was asking at the beginning of the day when she asked about the "garage door." So as he was on his way for a cup of coffee he stopped by her desk and asked:

"When my barn door was open, did you see my hummer parked in there?"

She smiled and replied, "No, I didn't. All I saw was an old minivan with two flat tires."

EDDY'S LAST WALK

Eddy Anderson was our mailman in the neighborhood for as long as I could remember. He was a nice guy and an integral part of the neighborhood. He would always buy Kool-Aid from our stand in the summers, played baseball with my old man and didn't talk down to us kids. He walked the walk for many years and when it was time to retire everyone in the neighborhood had a gift for him. He ended up with two bags that last day—one for the mail and the other for all the gifts he was getting! When he reached The Martin's house, Mrs. Martin was waiting on the porch for him. She was dressed in a sexy nightgown and when he went to give her the mail she took Eddy by the hand and led him into the house and up the stairs to bedroom. She pushed him back onto the bed, took off all of his clothes, climbed on top of him and proceeded to do the "Ooga Booga" with him. When they were done, she helped him get dressed and led him downstairs to the kitchen where she fed him the best breakfast he had ever had in his life. After he finished, Mrs. Martin said:

"Eddy look under your plate." Eddy lifted the plate and there was a dollar taped to it. "That's for you," she said and winked.

"You know, Mrs. Martin," Eddy replied, "I've been delivering your mail here for 24 years and you've never said a word to me in all those years. Now I come over and we go upstairs and do da "Ooga Booga" and you feed me the best breakfast I've ever had and then give me a dollar to boot. What the heck gives?"

"Well, when I was at the A&P, I overheard the women in the neighborhood talking about your retirement and how they were all gonna get you a gift. So, that night when my husband George came home from work I told him you were retiring and I was trying to figure out what kind of gift I should get you and he said, 'Screw 'em….give him a buck!' The breakfast was my idea."

———— ❧ ———————— ❧ ————

YOUR GRANDMA

Three of the toughest guys in Yooperland were sitting in Woody's Bar. Bucko Bonsai, an older man from the neighborhood stumbled in, sat down at the bar and ordered a drink. With his drink in hand, the older man spun around on his stool and scanned the bar. He spotted the three toughs in the corner and drunkenly wobbled over to their table. When he got there he put his hands on the table and leaned into the guy in front of him until he was almost next to his face.

"I went by your grandma's house and I saw her in the hallway stark naked. Man, she's fine!" The big tough stared back at Bucko but didn't say a word. His two friends looked at him puzzled as to why he didn't react at all to the old man.

"Hey! I got it on with your grandma and she gooooood. The best I've ever had!" Bucko continued. The tough just sat there stony face, taking the abuse. By this time his friends were getting irritated so they started nudging their friend to take action.

"I'll tell you something else, lad," Bucko sneered, "Your grandma loved it!" Finally the tough stood up and took Bucko by the shoulder and yelled:

"Dammit Grandpa! you're plastered, go home!"

THE BREWING ACCIDENT

Brenda Millimaki is home making dinner, when Arny, her husband's best friend shows up at the back door.

"May I come in? I got something to tell yah" Arny asks with his hat in his hand.

"Yah come on in, but where da heck is my husband at to?" Brenda asked, annoyed.

"That's what I'm here to tell yah," Arny says solemnly. "There was an accident down at da Bosch Brewery and Blinker is dead."

"Oh God no!" Brenda burst into tears. "How did it happen?"

"Well, it was bad. He fell into a vat of brew and drowned."

"Oh lord, oh lord, oh lord," Brenda lamented, "Tell me though Arny, did he at least go quickly?"

"Well no he didn't, actually." Arny said. "In fact, he got out three times to pee."

YOOPER BACHELOR

Long Nose Carlson was a long time yooper bachelor. One day his friend asked him:

"Why aren't you married yet? I can't believe you haven't found a good woman yet!"

"Actually," Long Nose said, "I've found a lot of girls that I've wanted to marry but when I bring them home to meet my folks, inevitably my ma doesn't like them!"

"Hmmm," his friend said, pondering a bit. "I think I've got the perfect solution. You need to find a girl who's just like your mother so she'll like them."

So, not long after, Long Nose meets a girl in Woody's Bar that reminds him of his mother to the tee. They start dating and six months after, he decides it's time to bring her home to meet his parents.

The next day, he goes over to his friend's house to tell him about it.

"Well, how did it go?" The friend asked.

"I did what you said," Long Nose said with his head hanging low. "I found the perfect girl. She's just like my ma and you were right, my mother absolutely loved her!"

"Why the long face then?"

Long Nose picked his head up. "Now my father doesn't like her!"

THE LAST SEND-OFF

A guy from the old neighborhood, Carly Jackson, passed away. Before he died, he had gotten all of his arrangements made and one of the things he wanted was for his favorite accordion player, Tommy Toumanen, to play some of Carly's favorite songs at the funeral. So we passed this information onto Tommy who agreed without to hesitation to fullfil his friend's last request.

On the day of the funeral, Tommy got waylaid by his barracuda of a mother-in-law and had to take her to WalMart to get her pills. By the time he got to the church he saw that he had missed the service. He felt bad and dejectedly walked out back to the cemetery to see if he could find where they were burying Carly. He finally saw Elmer Niemi and Bug-eyes Carlson shoveling dirt into a hole and thought, "Oh man, I'm not too late!"

"You guys don't mind if I play a few tunes do yah?" Tommy asked as he wiped down the ol' accordion.

"No, we don't mind, I guess," Bug-eyes said, a bit puzzled.

"Well old friend, I hope you enjoy these old tunes," Tommy said solemnly into the hole. He starts out with "Tick Tock Polka," one of Carly's favorites and then rips through "I Walk The Line" by Johnny Cash, then moves onto "I'm So Lonesome I Could Cry" by Hank Williams and finally ends with "Amazing Grace." Elmer and Bug-eyes were so touched by Tommy's renditions, they took their hats off and bowed when he was through. After Tommy thanked them and left Elmer turned to Bug-eyes and said:

"You Know, Bug-eyes, I've been putting in septic tanks for over 30 years and this the first time anything like this has ever happened!"

THE TEDDY BEAR COLLECTION

Fergie Aho was out prowling for men at Woody's Bar. She eventually meets Chick Mehan who was a stud from Tangle Town if there ever was one. They talk, they connect and at the end of the night they leave together. Chick takes her back to his place and shows her around his apartment. When they get to his bedroom, it's packed to the gills with sweet cuddly teddy bears. Hundreds of cute small bears on a low shelf, adorable medium sized ones on another shelf higher up and huge enormous bears on the very highest shelf.

Fergie was surprised to say the least. She couldn't believe that a man would have such an extensive collection of teddy bears but she just let it slide-- afterall, he was a very good looking guy and to tell the truth, she was a little impressed that he had a sensitive side to him.

After an intense night of passion, they are lying on Chick's bed in the afterglow, her throughly pleased with her sensitive lover, when she rolls over and asks him:

"Well how was it?" She twirled a little of his chest hair with her fingers.

Chick replies, "You can choose any prize you like from the bottom shelf."

SEEING-EYE DOG

Blind Eye Savolainen was standing on the corner of Oak and Spruce Street in Tangle Town with his seeing eye dog, Mortimer. As they were standing there waiting for the street light to change, the dog lifted his leg and peed on the Blind Eye's pant leg. He then reached into his pocket and took out a dog biscuit and gave it to the dog. U-Bolt Carlson, who had been watching this, tapped Blind Eye on the shoulder.

"You shouldn't do that you know. The dog'll never learn anything if you reward him when he does something like that." U-Bolt offered up.

"Oh I'm not rewarding him," Blind Eye said, "I'm just trying to find his head so I can kick him in the ass!"

THE MIRROR

Harold Finster's uncle Gorman lived deep in the woods of the Upper Peninsula for most of his life. One day he decided it was time to visit the big city of Marquette for the first time. While in town, he stops in at Walmart and after walking around the store in wide-eyed amazement, he picks up a mirror from the display and looks into it. Not knowing what it was, he says: "How about that, eh! Here's a picture of my daddy!" He bought "the picture" but on the way home he remembered his wife Olga didn't like his father. So he hung it in the shed and every morning before leaving for the woods, he would go out and look into the mirror.

Olga began to get suspicious of these morning trips to the woodshed. One day, after her husband left, she searched the barn and found the mirror and as she looked into the glass, she fumed, "So that's the old bitch he's running after!"

Old Age

A VISIT TO DOC PREVOST

I went to Doc Prevost for my yearly check up. After the exam, Doc Prevost says:

"Hoolie, you're doing fine. I don't see anything wrong with you physically . . . How are you doing mentally and emotionally? Do you got a good relationship with God?"

"Oh yah," I say, "me and God are real tight!"

"What do you mean, like, he answers your prayers?"

"Well, a little more than that. For instance, when I get up during the night to pee, when I get to the bathroom, I don't even have to do anything, he just turns the light on for me. When I'm done and I leave, POOF, he turns the light out for me!"

Doc Prevost sat for awhile after my story, stroking his chin and looking at me quizzically. Finally he said "O.K then Hoolie, sounds good. I'll see you soon," and started jotting in his notebook as I left his office. Well, unbeknownst to me, later in the day, he calls my wife Norm.

"Yeah, Norm, this is Doc Prevost calling. I just examined Hoolie and he's doing all right physically. But when I asked him about his mental state and if he was alright with God, he gave me a strange answer that I wanted to ask you about. He says when he goes to the bathroom at night, God turns on the light in the bathroom without having to do anything and when he's done and leaving the bathroom, God turns the light back out for him."

"Oh hell," Norm says, "that silly buggar's been peeing in the fridge again!"

GLEN AND UNCLE ERNIE

Glen Adams tells the story about his Uncle Ernie who was starting to lose it in his old age. He had to check on him everyday to make sure the old buggar was eating and generally not doing anything crazy. One day Glen makes his normal call to check in.

"Hello?" Uncle Ernie answers

"No, Glen's not here!" Uncle Ernie replies.

"No Uncle Ernie, this is Glen! Did you eat something today?"

"Yah, I fried up some potatoes and eggs for dinner."

"Didn't you eat that stew I left you yesterday?" Glen asked.

"Glen was supposed to stop by an bring me something to eat but he must've forgot."

"No I stopped by yesterday!"

"Who, Glen?" Uncle Ernie asked puzzled. "Oh you missed him he stopped by yesterday."

"No, Uncle Ernie," Glen said slapping his own forehead in frustration, "gee whiz this is Glen!"

"No, Glen Jr. isn't here, he's out driving truck."

"Oy. Anyways, well, what are you doing now?" Glen asked.

"Cuttin' wood and stackin' it."

"I told you to wait 'til I got there! I was gonna help you!"

"Yah, Glen said he was gonna help me with this wood but he never showed up!"

"Uncle Ernie, just sit dere, take it easy and eat that stew I brought you."

"Oh, I ate that stew yesterday." Uncle Ernie replied.

"Uncle Ernie please listen to me," Glen said, at the end of his rope. "This IS Glen. Do you need anything out dere before I come by?"

"I asked Glen to bring me out some butter and bacon and eggs but I haven't seen him yet."

"I brought that stuff yesterday, dang it! I put it in the fridge!"

"Yah well, can you bring me some butter and bacon and eggs?"

"Oh my god, O.K, Uncle Ernie, I'll bring that stuff out in an hour. How does that sound?"

"Yah that sounds real good, Glen, see you in an hour."

Glen gave himself another whack on the forehead before he hung up.

CRAZY DRIVERS

Arnold Maki puts on his coat and goes into the kitchen to talk to his wife.

"Eh, Martha, I gotta go doctor's down in Marquette today for a check up."

"Oh," she replies, "So you want me to drive you? You know how you're getting!"

"Drive me? What you think I'm senile? I've been driving for 50 years, I think I can drive to Marquette and back without losing my marbles, ya know!"

"O.K, O.K, but call if you get lost." Arnold leaves grumbling under his breath.

About 20 minutes after he leaves, Martha is doing the polka around the kitchen with her broom when the music is interrupted on the radio with an announcement.

"Ladies and Gentlemen, this is a warning for all you folks that are driving down U.S-41 towards Ishpeming. Apparently, there is a person driving on the wrong side of the highway. Please use caution if you're west bound towards Ishpeming."

Right away Martha dials Arnold on his cell phone.

"Arnold?"

"Yah it's me!"

"I just heard an announcement on the radio that some nutcase is driving down 41 the wrong way! Watch out for them, eh!"

"One nut?" Arnold replied. "Hell, dere's hundreds of 'em!"

THREE YOOPERS

Three old yoopers are sitting around playing cribbage at the Valenti Nursing Home. 75 year old Mutti says:

"You know, I get up at 6 in the morning to pee and I stand dere for half an hour and all that comes out is a little dribble. It's hell to get old!"

"Look at me," Carl says, "I'm 82 now and I get up at 7 a.m and sit on the toilet and after an hour and a half of gruntin' and groanin' I pass out a marble. Boy is it ever hell to get old! What about you Art?"

"Oh I tell you," Art says, "I'm pushing 90 and at 6 in the morning I pee like a race horse and at 7, I poop like a cow!"

"Well, eh," Carl replies, "that's pretty good for a guy your age!"

"Yah, well," Art says, "the trouble is, I don't wake up 'til 9!"

HONEY BEE

Honey Bee Anderson was getting up there in age. At the Valenti Nursing Home where she lived, she was known as the jokester and always loved to have a laugh. One day, she was walking down the hallway and she sees Leaf Olsen coming towards her.

"Hey Leaf, if you drop your drawers I bet you 5 bucks I can tell you how old you are!" Honey proposed.

"You're on dere, Honey Bee!" Leaf says and thinking he has this bet locked down, proceeds to drop his pants.

Honey takes a look at his johnson and replies, "You're 83 years old."

"Holy wah! How da hell can you tell that by looking at my mutton dagger?"

"Oh easy," Honey said, "You told me yesterday."

DA SNOWBIRDS

Me and my wife go out to Arizona for the winter coz we're sissy Yoopers who can't take the winters anymore. One of my friends who lives in the same trailer court as us, Charlie, is in great shape for his age. He's always hiking and biking to stay in shape. One day, he decided to take the run up 17 on his bike to Flagstaff.

"Holy wah!" I told him. "Those hills are going to kill you!"

"Nah," he replied, "I'm a cheesehead from Wisconsin, I'm tough. I'm going to have my wife meet me up in Flagstaff and drive me back."

I wished him luck and he took off. Everything was going fine until he started hitting all those steep hills. At one point he stopped his bike, totally worn out. A few minutes later a young guy in a Corvette pulls over and asks if everything is O.K.

"Yeah," Charlie replies, "I thought I could make this hill, but I ran out of steam."

"Well," the young dude replies, "If I had a roof rack, I could put your bike on top but I don't. I do have a rope though, so we could tie your bike to the car and I can pull you. I'll keep it around 30 m.p.h. I see you have that cool horn on your bike. Just honk it if I start going too fast."

So Charlie, ever the adventurer, agrees and they take off. Everything's going fine until another Corvette comes speeding up and pulls alongside the young guy's. The driver of the other Corvette looks at the young dude and points down the road indicating he wanted to race. Without hesitation, the young dude and his challenger gun it down the road.

Meanwhile, 5 miles up the road, a cop was sitting behind a billboard. His radio suddenly went off.

"Dave, it's Mike, you up there?" The radio squaks.

Dave presses his radio button. "Yeah I'm about 10 miles from you, behind the Safeway billboard."

"Well, you're not going to believe what's coming your way," Mike replied, "There's two Corvette's doing about 120 miles an hour. Here's the un-believable part. There's a guy on a pedal bike honking his horn trying to pass them!"

HAPPY HOUR

Four old retired guys are walking down a street in Apache Junction, Arizona. They turned a corner and a sign that says "Old Timer's Bar - All Drinks 20 Cents." They look at each other in disbelief and walk in thinking the sign is too good to be true.

"Come on in and let me pour one for you! What can I get you good sirs?" The old gentlemen behind the bar bellows to them across the bar. The guys approach the bar and seeing a well stocked bar, each orders a martini. Moments later, the bartender produces four iced martinis (dry, shaken not stirred) and says:

"That'll be twenty cents each please." The men stare at the bartender in amazement and then look at each other with a smile....they can't believe their good luck! They pay with the loose change they have in their pockets and once the first round is finished, they order another. Again, four excellent martinis are put in front of them and again they put their twenty cents on the bar for the drink. Finally one of the men couldn't handle his curiosity anymore and pipes up:

"Bartender, how can you afford to serve martinis as good as these for twenty cents a piece?"

"Well," the bartender replies, "I'm a retired tailor from Boston and I've always wanted to own a bar that harked back to a different era. Last year, I hit the jackpot in the lottery--125 million--and decided it was time to hang up my hat and follow my dream. Since I no longer want for money I decided to come down here with all the other retirees and serve all you fine folks drinks that everyone can afford!"

"What a great story!" One of the men said. "Here's to you bartender!" And they all raised their glass and continued to happily enjoy their martinis. A moment later, one of the guys noticed there were five guys sitting at the opposite end of the bar with no drinks in front of them, just staring forward in silence. Again, curious, one of the men asked: "What's with those guys down at the other end of the bar that are just sitting there?"

"Oh them," the bartender replied, "Those are a bunch of Yoopers from Michigan. They're all waiting for happy hour to start when drinks are half off!"

LIKE A NEWBORN BABY

Ray and Rudy were sitting on the porch at Valenti's Old Folks Home. They had been sitting in silence for some and in a moment of reflection, Ray turns to Rudy asks:

"Rudy, I'm 83 years old this year and I'm just full of aches and pains. I know you're about my age, how are you feeling?"

"Oh yah," Rudy replies after a beat, "Well, I feel like a newborn baby if you wanna know the truth!"

"Really!" Ray exclaims. "A newborn baby, eh? Well I'll Be!"

"Yah you betcha dere. I got no hair, no teeth and I think I just peed my pants!"

SILENT BUT DEADLY

Gracy and Buddy go to chuch one Sunday. Part way through the service, Gracy leans over and whispers in Buddy's ear:

"I've just let one rip but it was a silent one. What do you think I should do?"

Buddy whispers back, "I think you should put a new battery in your hearing aid!"

UNCLE LOU AND DA NURSING HOME

I took my Uncle Louie to the Valenti Nursing Home to let him check it out. He sat on the couch while I talked to the nurse in charge about the place. Uncle Louie started slowly leaning to the right and immediately a nurse came to his side and propped him up with a pillow. A minute later he started leaning to the left and almost immediately an orderly passing by propped him back up with a pillow. Another minute later he started leaning forward and the nurse who I was talking to ran over to him and put a pillow on his lap to help prop him back up.

After the visit with the nurse, I walked over to Louie on the couch all surrounded by pillows.

"Well Uncle Louie, how you like it so far?"

"It seems nice and clean and everyone that came by is real friendly. But—there's one thing I noticed . . ."

"What's that?" I asked.

"They won't let me fart."

DA DOC'S SOLUTION

Ben Talabaka goes to Doc Frounfelter, our local dentist, to get a check up on a tooth that was killing him.

"Well I gotta do a root canal," Doc says after his examination.

"Is it going to hurt?" Ben asked, worried.

"No, I'll just shoot you full of pain killers and you won't feel a thing."

"No way! I hate needles. What else you got?"

"I can give you gas."

"Naw, last time I had gas I got sicker than a dog. Anything else?"

"Well, I can give you one of these pills right here." Doc holds up a little blue pill.

"Whaddaya got there Doc?"

"It's Viagra."

"Oh," Ben says surprised. "Will it kill the pain?"

"No, but it will give you something to hang onto while you're screaming!"

CROSS COUNTRY TRIP

An elderly yooper couple, Barney and May, were driving across country. While May was behind the wheel, the two were pulled over by the highway patrol.

"Ma'am did you know you were speeding back there?" The officer asked when he got to the window.

May, hard of hearing, turned to Barney and asked, "What did he say?"

"He said you were speeding!" Barney yelled to May.

"May I see your license and registration?" The officer asked.

She turned to Barney again. "What did he say?"

"He wants to see your license and registration!" Barney yelled back.

May handed the officer her information. "I see you're from the U.P.," the patrolman said, "i spent some time there once and went out on a blind date with one of the ugliest women I've ever seen, poor creature."

"What did he say?" May turned to Barney once again.

"He said he knows you!" Barney barked back.

A BOWL OF ICE CREAM TO REMEMBER

Barker Neimi and his wife Sue were getting up there in age and in order to combat their old age forgetfulness, Doc Tobin suggested they write little notes to help them remember little day-to-day things.

One day, they were sitting in their living room watching TV when Sue pipes up. "Dear, will you please go to the kitchen and get me a bowl of ice cream? And make sure to write that down so you won't forget!"

"Nonsense!" Barker exclaimed. "I can remember a measly bowl of ice cream!"

"Well, I'd also like some fresh strawberries and whipped cream on it, so write that down!" Sue added.

"My memory's not that bad," Barker replied, "A bowl of ice cream with strawberries and whipped cream. See, I don't need to write that down."

"Oh I just rememebered—put some nuts on top too. C'mon, write this down, you'll forget!"

"No, no I won't forget. Ice cream, strawberries, whipped cream and nuts on top. I'll be right back with your treat, honey bunny."

For the next 15 minutes, Sue hears pots and pans banging around in the kitchen and she wonders what the hell Barker is up to in there. Finally Barker reappears and presents Sue with a plate of bacon and eggs.

"See, Barker, I knew you'd forget!" Sue yelled. "Where da heck is the toast I asked for?"

Chartered Trips

Rickets Maki and his wife Carla were vacationing in Florida and decided to take a charter boat out on the ocean. At one point they hit some rough waters and a massive wave crashed over the back of the boat where Rickets was and washed him out to sea. After an initial search turned up nothing, they brought Carla back to shore and sent out a search party. After three days, Carla received a fax from the boat at the front desk of the hotel. It read:

"Ma'am. Sorry to inform you that we found your husband dead at the bottom of the bay. We hauled him up to the deck and attached to his butt was an oyster and inside was a very rare pearl thought to be valued at 50,000 dollars. Please advise."

Carla dictated to the front desk clerk a response to the captain's fax.

"Sir. Send me the pearl and rebait the trap."

The Hearing Aid

Uncle Ernie, who couldn't hear for crap, went to Doc Tobin to get fitted for a hearing aid. Once the hearing aid was installed, Doc Tobin told him to come back in a month later for a follow up to see how it was working out and if they need to make any adjustments. After a month passed, Uncle Ernie came back in and Doc Tobin ran some tests.

"Judging from your tests, your hearing is almost fully restored with the hearing aid. Your family must be really happy that you can again, eh Ernie?"

"Oh I haven't told the family yet," Ernie replied solemnly. "I just sit around like normal pretending like I still can't hear and listening to the conversations. Let me tell you Doc, I've already changed my will three times dis month already!"

The Anniversary Present

Mukku was telling the guys at the mine that his 25th anniversary was coming up and he didn't know what to get Truna for a gift.

"I was thinking about getting her a new set of cast iron pans," Mukku said.

"No no no," Toivo retorted, "You gotta get her something sexy. Women like to still feel sexy even after 25 years of marriage. Trust me, I know." Mukku nodded solemnly, coz he knew Toivo was a yooper guru in all things.

So Mukku took a trip to da big city of Green Bay to find a gift for his beloved wife. He ended up at a Victoria's Secret like Toivo prompted him and went up to the sales lady.

"I've got my 25th anniversary coming up and I was looking to get my wife something real sexy," Mukku said bashfully.

"I know just the thing," the saleslady replied. She took Mukku over to a rack that had sheer see through nighties. "She'll absolutely love this one." So, Mukku, not knowing anything about lingerie, ponied up the 500 hundred bucks and had the sales lady wrap it up for him.

Back in Yooperland, just like both Toivo and saleslady said, Truna loved the gift.

"Why don't you go upstairs and put it on and model it for me," Mukku said. Truna ran upstairs still giddy from her gift. Once she was upstairs, she took the nighty out of the box and noticed the tag was still on it. 500 hundred bucks!

"Holy wah," she thought, "If I returned this, I could go on a screamer of a shopping trip in Green Bay! Hell, this thing is like wearing nothing anyways and Mukku's so blind he won't notice if I just go out there buck naked!" So she strips down to nothing and walks out to the top of the stairs.

"Well, what do you think of the gift you bought me? I just love it!" Truna asked with a little seductive wiggle.

Mukku takes a long look and shakes his head. "Gee whiz, for 500 bucks you'd think the least they could've done was iron all the wrinkles out!"

63

PLASTIC SURGERY EXPERIMENT

Ruth Talabaka goes down to Marquette to see Doc Tucklamaki, the plastic surgeon, to see if he can do something about her rapidly sagging face.

"You got two options," Doc said after his examination, "We can give you the old fashioned face lift or we can use a new hi-tech procedure called 'Da Knob.'"

"Oooo, what's 'Da Knob?'" Ruth asked, intrigued.

"It's a procedure where we install a knob under your hair on the back of your head. We then connect it to the facial muscles that sag and when you see new wrinkles and sagging, you just tighten the knob a few turns and your skin is nice and tight again."

"Oh yah," Ruth says nodding her head excitedly, "That's what I'd like. That 'Da Knob' procedure."

The next week Ruth goes under for her procedure and it turns out a complete success. She looked 15 years younger. As time went on, everytime she'd notice a new wrinkle or sag, she'd give the ol' knob a couple of twists and she was as good as new.

A couple years later, Ruth woke up and noticed huge bags under her eyes. It scared the crap outta her so she went in to see Doc Talabaka.

After examining her Doc gave his prognosis. "Well, Ruth, I think maybe you've overdone it on the knob twisting, because those bags under your eyes are your boobs."

"Holy Wah!" Ruth exclaimed. "I guess that explains my goatee!"

THE 80 YEAR OLD MAN

Hack Makkala walks out of Merrick's Drug Store in downtown Ishpeming and sees an older guy sitting on a bench crying.

"Are you OK, sir?" Hack asked.

"Oh yah," the old man replied, "It's my birthday today, I'm 82."

"Man, you look good for your age!"

"Thanks, young man. I just got married last week too!"

"Married?" Hack says surprised. "You old dog! You got your whole life ahead of you!"

"Yah, I married a 25 year old and we have sex everyday!" The old man said still sobbing.

"Man, oh man, you got it made! I'm lucky if I get it once a month! Tell me, it sounds like you've got it all. Why are you sitting here crying?"

"Well, you see that's the thing," The old man said tears streaming down his face, "I can't remember where I live…"

FRIED EGGS

Hack Harsala's wife Sauce was making a breakfast of fried eggs for him, much like she did the past 30 years of their marriage. Suddenly, Hack bursts into the kitchen and yells:

"Careful! Careful! Put in some more butter! Oh my god! You're cooking too many at once! Too many! Turn them! Turn them now! We need more butter, holy wah! Where are we going to get more butter? They're going to stick! Careful, now! See you never listen to me while you're cooking! Turn them, hurry up! Are you crazy? Have you lost your mind? Don't forget to salt them. You know you always forget to salt them—-"

"Holy wah, shut up already!" Sauce barked back. "What in the world is wrong with you? You think I don't know how to fry a couple of eggs?"

"Well," Hack replied, "I just wanted to show you what it feels like when I'm driving!"

NEW SUIT

Burt Neimi was moderately successful in his career as a mine boss at CCI. But as he got older, he found it harder and harder to go to work because of these incredible headaches he was getting. It was when his personal life started to suffer that he decided to finally seek medical help. After being referred from one specialist to another down in Marquette, he finally came across a doctor who solved his problem. His name was Dr. Ali Jem Leery.

"The good news is I can cure your headaches," said Doc Leery. "The bad news is it will require castration. You have a very rare condition that causes your testicles to press up against the base of your spine. The pressure on the spine is what's creating your bad headaches and the only way to relieve this pressure is to remove your testicles."

Burt was shocked and depressed. After pleading with the doctor to find another way and eventually seeking unsuccessful second opinions and with his headaches continuing, Bert reluctantly decided to go through with the operation.

Months after the procedure, his mind was finally free and clear of pain. He felt like a new person. One day as he was walking downtown Ishpeming, feeling particularly good, he passed Maki's Fine Men's Clothing Store. He paused for a moment at the window and thought: "You know, that's exactly what I need to match my new outlook on life: a new suit!"

He walked up to Elmer Maki, the house tailor and declared, "I'd like a new suit please, Elmer."

Elmer, with his expert eye, looked Burt up and down and stated matter of factly, "You're about a 44-Long."

Burt laughed. "That's amazing! You're right on the money. How did you know that?"

"It's my job to know that, Burt." Elmer replied. Burt tried on the suit that Elmer handed him. It fit perfectly. As he admired himself in the mirror, Burt continued. "How about a new shirt to go with that? You're about a 34 sleeve, 16 1/2 neck, correct?"

"How did you know that? You're right!" Burt exclaimed.

"As I said Burt, It's my job." Elmer handed him a fine, crisp white shirt and of course it fit perfectly. Burt was adjusting his collar in the mirror when Elmer asked him: "How about some new shoes? You got yourself a 9 1/2 wide," Elmer said eyeing his feet. Burt acquiesced and the shoes felt like a dream. "No suit is complete without a sharp hat," Elmer said grabbing a slick pork pie hat. "7 5/8, if I'm judging properly."

"Of course you are Elmer, you're a wizard at this stuff," Burt said slipping on the hat like a glove.

"You know, Burt, we just got these amazing designer Egyptian cotton underwear that you have to have. You want me to throw in a few pair with your ensemble?"

"Why not, sounds luxurious," Burt said as Elmer eyed his waist.

"Let's see—size 38 waist."

"A-ha!" Burt exclaimed. "You finally got one wrong! I've worn a size 34 since I was in my twenties!"

Elmer shook his head. "There's no way you're a size 34. If you did, it would press your gonads up against your spine and give you terrible headaches!"

THE OLD MAN AND HIS MOPED

At 25, Brill "Teacups" Rintamaki had sold his ingenious invention to a large corporation and was now a millionaire. The first thing he did was go out and buy the most expensive car he could think of--a brand new Ferrari 550. The first day he had it, he was feeling pretty cocky when he pulled up at a stop light next to Mungo Olsen, an elderly man from the neighborhood who was out for a buzz on his moped. Mungo looks over at the sleek, shiny car and asks, "What kind of car ya' got there, sonny?"

Teacups replies, "A Ferrari 550. It cost half a million dollars!"

"That's a lot of money," Mungo says. "Why does it cost so much?"

"Because this car can do up to 300 miles an hour easily!" Teacups states proudly.

"Mind if I take a look at her?" Teacups gestures for the old man to lean in and check it out. After surveying the interior of the car, Mungo leans back on his moped.

"That's a pretty nice car, all right...but I think I'll stick with my moped!"

Just then the light changes, Teacups decides to show the old man just what his car can do. He floors it, and within 30 seconds the speedometer reads 160 mph.

Suddenly, he notices a dot in his rear view mirror. It seems to be getting closer! He slows down to see what it could be and suddenly something whips by him in a blur.

"What on earth could be going faster than my Ferrari?!" Teacups asks himself. He floors the accelerator and takes the Ferrari up to 250 mph. Then, up ahead of him, he sees that it is in fact Mungo sailing along on his moped!

Amazed that the moped could pass his Ferrari, he gives it some more gas and passes the moped at 275 mph. He's feeling pretty good until he looks in his mirror and sees the old man gaining on him again. Astounded by the speed of this old guy he floors the gas pedal and takes the Ferrari all the way up to 300 mph. Not ten seconds later he sees the moped bearing down on him again. The Ferrari is flat out and there's nothing he can do.

Suddenly, the moped plows into the back of his Ferrari, demolishing the rear. The young man jumps out, and unbelievably, Mungo is still alive. He runs up to the mangled old man and says, "Oh my God! Is there anything I can do for you?"

Mungo wheezes in his dying breath, " Yah you can unhook my suspenders from your side-view mirror!"

Shirley

You Should See Da Udder Guy

Shirley Antilla was a tough old babe that lived in my hood. She had a gruff, deep voice from too many ciggies and could out-work, drink or fight any man. One day, I saw her walking on the street and she had on a pair of sunglasses that were obviously hiding two black eyes which you could still see peeking out around the edges of the glasses.

"Holy wah, what happened to you?" I asked.

"Me and Blue Jay [her husband] got into a scrape last night. Hell, you think I look bad, you should see him!"

Follow Da Snowplow

When Shirley opened the doors at Shopko to go outside after work, it was snowing heavily and blowing to the point that visibility was almost zero. As she sat in her car letting it warm up, she wondered how she was going to get home. She finally remembered her husband's advice that if she got caught in a blizzard she should wait for a snow plow to come by and follow it. Confident in her plan she waited until she saw the familiar flashing yellow lights cutting through the swirling haze and felt the low rumble of the snow plow. She pulled out and caught up with the snow plow, making sure to keep a safe distance. Shirley was so pleased that her plan was working out well that she almost didn't notice that the plow had suddenly pulled to a stop. She pulled in behind the truck and was waiting for the truck to continue its route, when to her surprise she saw faintly in the haze the figure of the snowplow driver walking towards her car. She rolled down the window when he finally reached her.

"Are you alright m'am?" The driver asked.

"Oh I'm fine young man. My husband Blue Jay told me that if I was ever in a bad storm like this the safest way was to follow a snowplow."

"Well, that's OK with me, but I just wanted to let you know that I'm almost done with the Shopko parking lot here and then I'm headed over to K-Mart next."

Word On Da Street

The word around the neighborhood was that Shirley's husband Blue Jay had died. I went over to see her to give her my support. When I found her, she was in the backyard garden digging a hole. I went up to her and gave her a hug.

"I'm so sorry about Blue Jay," I consoled.

"Hoolie, don't worry about me, I couldn't stand the cheap bugger. I had to put up with his crap for so many years . . . I had dat bugger cremated you know. Then d'yknow what I did? I took some of his ashes and mixed them up with dat 'mari-ju-wannah' and smoked it! And you know what? That was the best he's made me feel in 30 years!"

Who's Da Dummy?

The VFW had a ventriloquist performing one night and the place was packed. He was going through his act and everyone was really laughing and having a great time. Then, toward the end of the act he started telling some "dumb blonde" jokes. All of a sudden from the back of the room Shirley, offended because of her honey yellow blonde hair, starts yelling at him.

"What's wrong wit you anyhow?" She barked. "Just because I got blonde hair you saying I'm stupid? There's a lot of blondes that are pretty damn smart, don'cha'know? You're nothing but a bigot saying that all blondes are dumb!"

The ventriloquist caved. "I'm sorry m'am, I never meant to insult your intelligence. My wife is blonde and she went to Harvard Law School."

"Hey," Shirley yelled back, "I'm not talking to you. I'm talking to that little weasel sittin' on your lap!"

WHAT HAPPENS IN VEGAS

Blue Jay comes home and sees Shirley is packing her suitcase. "Where are you off too, then?" He asks.

"Las Vegas." Shirley replies. "I found out dere are guys who will pay me 400 bucks a pop to do what I do to you for free!"

Blue Jay starts packing his bag alongside hers. "Where da heck do you think you're going?" Shirley asks.

"I'm going out to Las Vegas with you. I want to see how you're going to live off of 400 dollars a year."

SCENT BIRD

Shirley steps onto the elevator at the Bellagio in Vegas to go up to her room. Just as she presses the button to her room, two well dressed ladies about her age step into the elevator and as they eye Shirley's discount threads, put their nose up in the air and scooch as far away as they can from her. After a moment of awkward silence one of the ladies turns to the other and asks:

"Oooo, whatever is that scent you're wearing, it's just divine!"

"Oh, that," the first lady says as she looks sideways at Shirley. "That's Georgio Armani, a hundred dollars an ounce. And what about yours? I've been meaning to ask you all day."

"Well," the second lady says casting Shirley a look, "That's Chanel Number 5, a hundred and fifty dollars an ounce." Just then the elevator dings on Shirley's floor. The doors open and as Shirley is walking out, she lifts her leg and rips a loud and equally fowl fart at the women.

"Broccoli, IGA, forty-nine cents a pound," She says as she walks away.

SHIRLEY AND GERTIE

Shirley and Gravel Gertie were sitting at Hickeys Bar. Shirley says to Gertie: "Boy, Gertie your skin looks so nice compared to my leathery looking skin and its so soft. How you get your skin to look like this?"

"Well," Shirley replied, "Once a week I fill da bathtub up with milk and soak in it for a coupla hours."

"Where you go to get dat much milk?" Gertie asked.

"I just go out and see Elmer Aho out at his farm. He's always got plenty."

The next day, Shirley, excited to start her skin care regiment goes out to Aho's farm to see Elmer, who was standing by his cow fence when she pulled up.

"Oh Elmer, I need some milk."

"How much you need dere Shirley?"

"Enough to put in my bathtub to soak in."

"Pasterized?"

"No, just up to my boobs."

MORE SHIRLEY AND GERTIE

Shirley and Gravel Gertie were taking the dirt roads back to town from the Pine Grove Bar because they were both loaded to the gills and wanted to avoid the cops. All of a sudden, a car pulls out of an old bush road with its lights flashing.

"Oh hell," Shirley said, "Its that damn bloody local cop again! I swear this got to be hundredth time he's pulled us over!"

Once they pulled over, the cop walks up to their car and unzips his fly.

"Oh crap," Shirley turned to Gertie, "He's gonna make us take dat yooper breath-a-lizer test again!"

SHIRLEY AND BLUE JAY

It came time for Shirley and Blue Jay to celebrate their 30 years of marriage. Blue Jay asks her:

"There's been something bothering me for awhile. We've got 12 kids, each as wonderful as the last. But that Mukku of ours has always stood out as the oddball. He doesn't look like the rest of the kids and it's made me wonder; have you ever cheated on me in our 30 years? Answer honestly, after all this time, I'll forgive you."

"Well, if it's honesty you want, Carl," Shirley replies, "Then yes, I cheated on you. Mukku is your real son."

SHIRLEY AND DA BIKERS

Shirley knocked on the door to the local biker's club looking to join. A big hairy bearded biker with tattoos all over his arms answers the door.

"Yah, what you want, granny?" He says gruffly.

"I wanna join your biker's club," Shirley replied.

The biker chuckled. "You gotta meet certain requirements before you're allowed to join. First, you got a bike?"

"Yah, that's my Harley over there."

"Oh, yah that's a nice bike. Second, do you smoke?"

"Yah," Shirley replied, "I smoke two packs of camels a day and cigars when I'm shootin' pool."

The biker, obviously impressed so far, continued. "Most importantly, have you ever been picked up by The 'Fuzz?'"

"No, I've never been picked up by the fuzz but I've been swung around by my nipples a few times!"

THE GREAT CRISLA-MAKI

Shirley visited local psychic The Amazing Crisla-maki to get her fortune read. In a dark and hazy room, Crisla-maki appeared to go into a trance as he waved his hands around his crystal ball and after a moment he said in a forboding voice:

"Sometime in the next year, you must prepare yourself to become a widow, Mrs. Maki. Your husband will die a violent and horrible death."

Visibly shaken, Shirley stared at the psychic's lined face, then at the single flickering candle, then down at her hands. She took a few deep breaths to compose herself.

"Well," Shirley asked, voiced quivering, "Will I at least be acquitted?"

---

911 CALL

A couple of hunters from Detroit are out hunting deer north of Ishpeming when one of them falls to the ground. His friend runs over to him and found that his eyes were rolled in the back of his head and he didn't appear to be breathing. Without hesitation, he whips out his cell phone and calls 911.

Shirley was working the switchboard when they called. She heard the hunter gasp: "I think my friend is dead! What can I do?"

Shirley with her calm, soothing yooper voice says, "Just take it easy der chum. I can help yah. First, let's make sure the bugger's dead, eh!" There was a silence and then she hears a gunshot go off through the phone. After awhile the mittenhead comes back on the line.

"OK, he's dead, now what?"

THE SALES POSITION

Because jobs are sparse here in the U.P, sometimes Yoopers are forced to move away from their beloved home and find oppourtunity in bigger cities. After getting laid off as a 911 operator, Shirley had to pull up stakes and head to Milwaukee to look for work. She had always wanted to work in sales and soon found a department store that was looking for salespeople. Shirley charmed her way in, despite her lack of experience and at the end of her first day, the boss came up to her.

"So how many sales did you make today?" He asked.

"Just one." Shirley said confidently.

"One?" The boss said visually disappointed. "I know this is your first day but most of our sales people make at least 20 sales per day, even on a slow day! How much was the sale worth?"

"Exactly one hundred thousand, three hundred forty-three dollars and fifty three cents." Shirley replied.

"How did you manage THAT!" The boss asked flabbergasted.

"Well, dis guy came in and I sold him a small fish hook, then a medium fish hook and finally a really large hook. Then I sold him a small fishing line, a medium one and a huge one. I asked him where he was going fishing and he said he was going up to Oscoda to fish Lake Huron. I said he'd probably need a boat, so I took him down to the boat department and sold him the fancy 22-foot Chris Craft with twin engines. Then he said his Honda Civic probably wouldn't be able to handle the load, so I took him to the vehicle department and sold him a new GMC 1-ton pick-up truck."

"You sold all that to a guy who came in for a fish hook?" The boss asked who still couldn't believe what he was hearing.

"Nah he didn't come in for a fish hook," Shirley replied, "He came in to buy a box of tampons for his wife and I said to him, 'Your weekend's shot. You might as well go fishing.'"

Roy Boy

TALKING CLOCK

Roy Boy was proudly showing off his new apartment to friends late one night. Half bagged, he led the way to his bedroom where there was a big brass gong.

"What's the big gong for?" Eddy asked.

"Ahh, that's my talking clock," Roy Boy replied, a little tipsy on his feet.

"How does it work?"

"Watch this," Roy Boy said, giving it an earth shattering pound with the hammer. Suddenly, someone on the other side of screamed:

"FOR GOD'S SAKE, YOU IDIOT, KNOCK IT OFF IT'S 2 A.M IN THE BLOODY MORNING!"

THE AFFAIR

Roy Boy was having an affair with his secretary Grace. One day at her place, after a particularly steamy encounter, Roy Boy fell asleep and jolted awake around 8 PM. He frantically threw on his clothes and told Grace to take his shoes outside and rub them through the grass and dirt. Mystified, she nonetheless did what he asked and returned his shoes to him. Once home, his wife was waiting at the kitchen table.

"Where the hell have you been, I've been calling you all night!" She demanded.

"Darling," Roy Boy replied, "I can't lie to you. I've been having an affair with my secretary Grace. I fell asleep in her bed and didn't wake up until a half hour ago."

His wife looked him up and down and stopped at his shoes. "Oh right, tell me another one, loverboy! You've been out golfing again haven't you?"

THE MONASTERY

After a long day of fishing, Roy Boy decided to pack it in when it started raining buckets. It got so bad at one point, he decided to pull over at a monastery deep in the woods of Yooperland to wait out the storm. The monks invited him inside for dinner and to stay the night if he liked. That night, they served up what was the greatest fish and chips Roy Boy had ever had in his life. Full and completely satisfied after the meal, he decided to compliment the chef and see if he could get a couple of secrets out of him.

In the kitchen, Roy Boy found a short, portly man sweeping the floor. "Are you the fish frier?" He asked.

"No," the man replied, "I'm the chip monk."

THE EULOGY

Maria, Roy Boy's cousin and a devout Catholic, got married and had 10 children. Her husband died young and eventually she remarried. She had another 7 kids with her second husband, who also died before his time. Not long after her second husband died, Maria also passed away. At her funeral, with her 17 kids lined up in the front row and her sister, who was now in charge of the brood, the priest looked skyward and raised his hands and said:

"At last they are together."

Her sister, between sobs piped up, "Excuse me, Father but do you mean she and her first husband or she and her second husband?"

The priest replied, "No, I was referring to her legs."

CAMPFIRE STORIES

Mike, Tubba and Roy Boy were sitting around the campfire telling stories. The question was asked "What was the worst thing that's ever happened to you." Mike went first.

"I was hitch-hiking on a dark road one night and a bus came along and ran me over. I broke my back and wound up in the hospital for nearly a year." They all nodded in sympathy to Mike's tale of woe. Then Tubba pipes up.

"We were working a construction job in Milwaukee and I was on some scaffold seven stories up when the scaffold collapsed and I fell, breaking every bone in my body on the way down. I ended up in the hospital for 6 months!" Mike and Roy Boy winced and shook their head at their friend's story.

"Your turn Roy Boy." Mike said.

Roy Boy thinks for a bit and then says, "Well, I'll tell you about the second worst thing to happen to me. I was out hunting one time and I had to take a dump, so I stepped behind some bushes, dropped my hunting pants and crouched down." Roy Boy paused.

"Yah….and then what happened?" Tubba said in anticipation.

"I got a little too close to the ground and WHAM! A bear trap snapped shut on my gonads. I never howled so loud in my life or ran so quickly!"

"God!" Mike exclaimed, "If that's the second worst thing, what could possibly be worse than that?"

"Oh, well," Roy Boy replied, "That would be when I reached the end of the chain."

THE DEBT

Roy Boy was getting into the shower just as his wife Marge was finishing up when the door bell rang. She quickly wraps herself in a towel and runs downstairs. When she opens the door she sees Bill Bob, the next door neighbor. Bill Bob eyes Marge in her towel and flashes a grin:

I'll give you 800 bucks to drop your towel," he says, beaming. He produces a wad of cash out of his pocket. After mulling it over for a moment,

Marge shrugs her shoulders and drops her towel. Bill Bob's eyes get really huge and for a few moments gapes at Marge like a little boy in a candy shop. While still in a trance, he hands Marge the wad of cash and she shuts the door with him still standing there. Back upstairs, Roy Boy was just getting out of the shower.

"Who was that?" he asked.

"It was just Bill Bob from next door," she replied.

"Oh," Roy Boy said as he poked his head out of the bathroom, "Did he say anything about the 800 bucks he owes me?"

FERTILITY TREATMENT

Roy Boy and his wife were trying to have a kid but it wasn't working. So, Doc Tobin wanted to first see what Roy's sperm count was. He gave him a jar and told him to bring back a semen sample tomorrow. The next day, Roy Boy came back and handed the doc the jar which was clean and empty as when he gave it to him.

"What happened, Roy?" Doc asked.

"Well Doc, it's like this. First, I tried my right hand but nothing. Then I tried with my left hand but still, nothing. Then I asked da wife for help, she tried with her right hand, then with her left and still, nothing. She tried with her mouth, first with her teeth in, then with them out. Nothing. We even called up da neighbor lady and she tried too, first with both hands, then an armpit—hell, she even tried squeezing it between her knees!"

The Doc laughed. "I can't believe you asked the neighbor lady for help with something like that! Marge allowed that?"

"Well yah," Roy Boy said, "Marge didn't mind, she even watched."

"What??" The Doc exclaimed, confused.

"Yah, well, when neither of us could get that damn lid off the jar, we figured we'd let her have a go at it…"

THE AFFAIR PT. 2

Roy Boy's wife Marge is laying in bed with Roy's best friend, Cranker Carlson, when the phone rings. Marge picks up the receiver and Cranker listens to the one sided conversation.

Marge spoke with an over the top cheery voice. "Hello? Oh hi! I'm so glad you called. Really? That's wonderful. I'm so happy for you, that sounds terrific! Great, thanks. Okay, bye bye!" Marge hangs up the phone.

"Who was that?" Cranker asked.

"Oh," Marge replies, "that was Roy Boy telling me all about the wonderful time he's having on his deer hunting trip with you."

WEDDING NIGHT

Roy Boy was with his buddies in the bar. They were all bragging about what kind of control they had over their wives but Roy Boy was silent. After awhile, Boosta turns to Roy and says:

"Well, what about it, Roy? What kind of control do you have over your wife?"

"Well, let's see," Roy Boy says with confidence, "On our honeymoon I made damn sure Marge came to me on her hands and knees!"

"Woah, what happened then?" Boosta asked with excitement.

"Well," Roy said as he sank down in his chair, "Then she said 'Get the hell out from under that bed and fight like a man!'"

A NIGHT TO REMEMBER

Roy Boy was drinking at Woody's Bar. At one point he stood up unsteadily and stumbled to the bathroom. He was in there awhile and periodically the people in the bar could hear him yelping. after 5 or 6 yelps, the bartender,

"Quarter To Three" Johnson reluctantly went to the bathroom door to check on Roy Boy.

"Roy, what are you yelling about in there? You're scaring the customers!"

"Well you see," Roy responded, "I was taking a dump and everytime I try to flush the toilet, something keeps biting my gonads!"

"Oh brother," Quarter To Three rolled his eyes, "Roy, get off the mop bucket already whydon'cha?"

THE BURGLER

FINLAND CALLING

Roy Boy takes a trip to Finland to see his distant relatives. He was sad to be apart from his beloved cat Bootsie but his wife Marge told him she would take real good care of her. As soon as he landed in Finland he called his wife to check on the cat.

"How's little Bootsie doing?" He asked.

"Oh, Roy Boy," Marge said solemly, "Your cat's dead."

"Oh god!" Roy Boy said in despair. "Did you have to tell it to me that way? It's so harsh!"

"Well how else am I supposed to tell you your cat's dead?" Marge asked puzzled.

"You should have lead up to it gradually. For instance, you could've told me Bootsie was on the roof but the fire department is getting it down at the moment. Then when I called later you could've said that when they tried to get her, she jumped off the roof and broke her back but our vet is doing everything he can to save her. Then when I called the next day, you could've said the vet did all he could but Bootsie passed away in surgery. That way I could've been prepared and it wouldn't be such a shock."

"By the way," Roy Boy continued, "How's my mother doing?"

After a pause Marge said, "Your ma? Oh yah, well she's up on the roof but the fire department is getting her down at the moment...."

THE HORSE

Roy Boy was reading the latest issue of The Mining Journal one morning when his wife Marge walks up behind him and smacks him alongside the head with her cast iron frying pan (a yooper woman's weapon of choice).

"What da heck was that for?" Roy Boy asked rubbing his head.

"I found a matchbook in your pocket with 'Betty Sue' written on it."

"Holy wah, Margie," Roy Boy replied still rubbing his head. "Remember last week when I went to the track? 'Betty Sue' was the name of the horse that I bet on!" Satiated but still suspicious, Marge shrugged her shoulders with an "OK, Buster" and walked away.

Three days later, Roy Boy is once again reading the paper at the kitchen table when Marge walks up behind him and smacks him in the head with the frying pan once more.

Roy Boy jumps up this time and yells, "Again with the frying pan! What is with you, woman?"

Marge gives Roy a look that could kill and said, "Your damn horse just called."

Fredric's Of Ironwood

Roy Boy's wife Marge decided she wanted to do something special to please Roy Boy when he came home from his hunting trip. So, she bought a pair of crotchless panties from the Fredric's of Ironwood catalog. That night when he got home, Roy Boy walked into the bedroom to find his wife sprawled on the bed, spread eagle.

"Hi honey," she purred in a seductive voice. "Come and get some of this!"

"God no!" Roy Boy roared. "Look at what it did to your undies!"

Out For A Drive

Roy Boy and Marge were out driving one day when a state cop pulled him over.

"What seems to be the problem, dere, eh?" Roy Boy asked.

"Sir," the cop replied, "didn't you notice that your wife fell out of the car back there?"

"Oh thank god you told me that," Roy Boy said wiping his brow. "For awhile there I thought I was deaf!"

The Genie Of South Beach

Roy Boy was walking on South Beach along Lake Superior when he stumbled across an old lamp. He picked it up and rubbed the sand off of it and lo and behold, a yooper genie popped out.

"Ok you got me out of dat bottle," says the genie, "Thanks, eh. I'm a Yooper genie so I can only grant you one wish."

Roy Boy thought about it for awhile and said, "I've always wanted to go to Hawaii but I'm too scared to fly and I get sick if I go on a boat. Could you build me a bridge to Hawaii so I can drive over there to visit?"

The genie laughed and replied, "That's impossible! Think of the logistics of that! How would the supports ever reach the bottom of the Pacific? Think of all the concrete and all of the steel that would take! Think of something else, eh!"

Roy Boy was visibly disappointed but in the end said, "OK, I'll try and think of something real good," and after a moment, "I've been married and divorced four times. My wives always said that I don't care and that I'm insensitive so, I wish that I could understand women, know how they feel inside and what they're thinking when they give me the silent treatment, know why they're crying, know what they really want when they say 'nothing,' know how to make them truly happy."

The yooper genie replies, "So—do you want that bridge to be two lanes or four?"

Diary of
a Yooper
Transplant

The following is an exerpt from the diary of a transplant's (from Detroit) first winter in the U.P.

December 9th: We woke to a beautiful blanket of crystal white snow covering every inch of the landscape. What a fantastic sight! Can there be a more lovely place in the whole world? Moving to Yooperland from Detroit was the best idea I've ever had. I shoveled snow for the first time in years and it made me feel like a boy again! I did both our driveway and the sidewalks. This afternoon the snow plow came along and covered up the sidewalks and closed the driveway, so I got to shovel again! What a perfect life!

December 12th: The sun has melted our lovely snow. Such a disappointment. My neighbor tells me not to worry, we'll definitely have a white Christmas. No snow on Christmas would be awful! Bob says we'll have so much snow by the end of winter, that I'll never want to see snow again. I don't think that's possible. Bob is such a nice guy—I'm glad he's our neighbor.

December 14th: Snow, lovely snow! Eight inches last night. The temperature dropped to 20 below. The cold makes everything sparkle so. The wind took my breath away but I warmed up by shoveling the driveway and sidewalks. This is the life! The snow plow came back this afternoon and buried everything again. I didn't realize I would have to do quite this much shoveling but I'll certainly get back in shape this way. I wish I wouldn't huff and puff so much.

December 15th: 20 inches forecast. Sold my van and bought a 4x4 Blazer. Bought snow tires for the wife's car and two extra shovels. Stocked the freezer. The wife wants a wood stove in case the electricity goes out. I think that's silly. We aren't in Alaska, after all.

December 16: Ice storm this morning. Fell on my butt in the driveway trying to salt the ice. Hurt like hell. The wife laughed for an hour, which was very cruel.

December 17th: Still way below zero. Roads are too icy to go anywhere. Electricity was off for five hours. I had to pile the blankets on to stay warm. Nothing to do but stare at the wife and try not to irritate her. Guess I should've bought a wood stove but won't admit it to her. God I hate it when she's right.

I can't believe I'm freezing to death in my own living room.

December 20th: Electricity's back on but had another 14 inches of stupid snow last night. More shoveling. Took all day. That stupid snow plow came by twice. Tried to find a neighbor kid to shovel but they said they're too busy playing hockey. I think they're lying. Then called the only hardware store in Ishpeming to see about buying a snow blower and they're out. Might have another shipment in March. I think they're lying. Bob says I have to shovel or the city will have it done and bill me. I think he's lying.

December 22nd: Bob was right about a white Christmas because 13 more inches of the white stuff fell today and it's so cold it probably won't melt until August. Took me 45 minutes to get dressed up to go out to shovel and then I had to use the bathroom. By the time I got undressed and dressed back up, I was too tired to shovel. Tried to hire Bob who has a plow on his truck for the rest of the winter but he says he's too busy. I think that jerk is lying.

December 23rd: Only two inches of snow today. And it warmed up to zero! The wife wanted me to decorate the front of the house this morning. What is she, nuts? Why didn't she tell me to do that a month ago? She says she did but you know, I think she's lying.

December 24th: Six inches today. Snow packed so hard by snow plow, I broke the shovel. Thought I was having a heart attack. If I ever catch the jerk who drives the plow, I'll drag him through the snow by his hair! I know he hides around the corner and waits for me to finish shoveling and then he comes down the street at about 100 miles an hour and throws snow all over where I've just been. Tonight the wife wanted me to sing Christmas carols with her and open presents but I was too busy watching for that stupid snow plow.

December 25th: Merry Christmas, 20 more inches of snow! Snowed in. The idea of shoveling makes my blood boil. God I hate snow! Then the snow plow driver came by asking for a donation and I hit him over the head with my shovel! The wife said I had a bad attitude. I think she's an idiot. If I have to watch "It's a Wonderful Life" one more time I'm going to kill her.

December 26th: Still snowed in. Why the hell did I ever move here? It was all her idea. She's really getting on my nerves.

December 27th: Temperature dropped to 30 below and the pipes froze.

December 28th: Warmed up to above 50 below! Still snowed in. That woman is driving me crazy!

December 29th: Ten more inches. Bob says I have to shovel the roof or it could cave in. That's the silliest thing I ever heard. How dumb does he think I am?

December 30th: Roof caved in. The snow plow driver is suing me for a million dollars. The wife went home to her mother. Nine inches predicted.

December 31st: Set fire to what's left of the house. No more shoveling!!

January 8th: I feel so good! I just love those little white pills they keep giving me! Why am I tied to the bed? Happy New Year!

———————————————————

YOOPER INNOVATIONS, INC
490 N. STEEL ST.
ISHPEMING, MI 49855
800.628.9978
ANNA@DAYOOPERS.COM